Advanced Introduction to Behavioral Finance

Elgar Advanced Introductions are stimulating and thoughtful introductions to major fields in the social sciences, business and law, expertly written by the world's leading scholars. Designed to be accessible yet rigorous, they offer concise and lucid surveys of the substantive and policy issues associated with discrete subject areas.

The aims of the series are two-fold: to pinpoint essential principles of a particular field, and to offer insights that stimulate critical thinking. By distilling the vast and often technical corpus of information on the subject into a concise and meaningful form, the books serve as accessible introductions for undergraduate and graduate students coming to the subject for the first time. Importantly, they also develop well-informed, nuanced critiques of the field that will challenge and extend the understanding of advanced students, scholars and policy-makers.

For a full list of titles in the series please see https://www.elgaronline.com/ , and https://www.advancedintros.com/ for Elgar Advanced Introduction in Law.

Advanced Introduction to

Behavioral Finance

H. KENT BAKER
University Professor of Finance, Kogod School of Business, American University, USA

JOHN R. NOFSINGER
Dean and William H. Seward Chair in International Finance, College of Business and Public Policy, University of Alaska Anchorage, USA

VICTOR RICCIARDI
Instructor of Finance, College of Business, Tennessee Tech University, USA

Elgar Advanced Introductions

 Edward **Elgar**
PUBLISHING

Cheltenham, UK • Northampton, MA, USA

Published by
Edward Elgar Publishing Limited
The Lypiatts
15 Lansdown Road
Cheltenham
Glos GL50 2JA
UK

Edward Elgar Publishing, Inc.
William Pratt House
9 Dewey Court
Northampton
Massachusetts 01060
USA

A catalogue record for this book
is available from the British Library

Library of Congress Control Number: 2023936962

Printed on elemental chlorine free (ECF)
recycled paper containing 30% Post-Consumer Waste

ISBN 978 1 80220 698 2 (cased)
ISBN 978 1 80220 699 9 (eBook)
ISBN 978 1 80220 700 2 (paperback)

Printed and bound in the USA

To Linda and Rory – H. Kent Baker
To Anna, my wife and best friend – John R. Nofsinger
To Lorraine and Jeff Lunt – Vic Ricciardi

Contents

Abbreviations

2D:4D	ratio between the length of the second and fourth fingers
AAII	American Association of Individual Investors
AIM	affect infusion model
AMH	adaptive markets hypothesis
APT	arbitrage pricing theory
BCF	behavioral corporate finance
BLCT	behavioral life-cycle theory
BPT	behavioral portfolio theory
BPV	behavioral-adjusted present value
CAPM	capital asset pricing model
CEO	chief executive officer
CFO	chief financial officer
CPT	cumulative prospect theory
CRT	cognitive reflection test
CSR	corporate social responsibility
DCF	discounted cash flow
DPS	dividends per share
EA	education attainment
EMH	efficient market hypothesis
EUT	expected utility theory
fMRI	functional magnetic resonance imaging
GWAS	genome-wide association studies
HRS	Health and Retirement Study

IPO	initial public offering
IQ	intelligence quotient
IRA	individual retirement account
IRR	internal rate of return
LCH	life-cycle hypothesis
LCT	life-cycle theory
M&A	merger and acquisition
MMH	mood maintenance hypothesis
MPT	modern portfolio theory
NPV	net present value
OECD	Organisation for Economic Co-operation and Development
PAPM	popular asset pricing model
PT	prospect theory
RMET	Reading the Mind in the Eyes Test
SEU	subjective expected utility
SMT	Save More Tomorrow
SNPs	single nucleotide polymorphisms
SRI	socially responsible investing
TPB	theory of planned behavior
TSP	Thrift Savings Plan
TV	television
WCM	working capital management

1   A behavioral alternative emerges to standard finance

Behavioral finance sits at the crossroads of finance, economics, psychology, social psychology, decision-making, science and neurology, to name but a few of the disciplines that make up its strange brew.
–Daniel Crosby (2014, p. 49)

Introduction

The birth of behavioral finance, a subfield of behavioral economics, stems from early attempts to bring psychology into finance (Shefrin, 2001a). One area focused on explaining various anomalies. In economics and finance, an *anomaly* is when an actual result using a given set of assumptions differs from the expected result predicted by a model. An anomaly suggests that a specific assumption or model does not hold in practice. Thaler (2015, p. 347) notes, "Much to everyone's surprise, the behavioral approach to economics has had its greatest impact in finance."

Many proponents of modern finance initially ignored, denied, or tried to nullify the outpouring of behavioral finance research. The defensive posture of the traditionalists was unsurprising given that the scholarly research in behavioral finance often differed markedly from established theories and perspectives. A succession of discoveries from behavioral finance researchers eroded the faith in the basic tenets of standard finance (Shiller, 2003) and drew attention to the psychological dimensions of financial behavior. Eventually, the momentum of this new paradigm took hold, and the controversy surrounding behavioral finance subsided, resulting in its growing acceptance by academics, industry executives, and policymakers. Additionally, interest in behavioral finance led many to rethink their assumptions and models.

This chapter traces the evolution of academic finance, including the emergence of behavioral finance. It then addresses some early behavioral finance theories and psychological concepts that scholars developed during its formative years (i.e., generally before the 2000s).

The evolution of academic finance

The history of finance and finance-related activities begins with the dawn of civilization. *Finance* deals with raising, spending, investing, and managing money. *Economics* concerns the production, consumption, and distribution of goods and services to explain how economies work and people interact. Its two main branches are macroeconomics, focusing on the overall economy, and microeconomics, dealing with specific economic factors. Although economics and finance are separate disciplines, they are interrelated and influence each other (Simpson, 2021).

In the 1940s and 1950s, finance arose as a distinct field from economics to study theory and practice. Finance's three main categories are public, corporate, and personal finance. However, other subcategories emerged over time, like behavioral and social finance (Hayes, 2021). *Behavioral finance* seeks to identify the psychological, cognitive, emotional, and social reasons underlying financial decisions. *Social finance* is an approach to managing investments that generate financial returns while including measurable positive social and environmental impacts.

Standard finance

Before behavioral finance emerged, finance had evolved from the "old finance," focusing on analyzing financial statements and the nature of financial claims, to "modern finance," centering on valuation based on rational economic behavior (Haugen, 2002). In economics, *rational* means people are consistent in their behavior. Economic theories and models assume that people typically have distinct preferences and make well-informed, self-interested decisions based on those preferences. Hence, people are efficient and unbiased processors of relevant information and make decisions consistent with utility maximization.

In the 1950s and 1960s, business schools started teaching some concepts of modern finance, also now called conventional, standard, and traditional finance. Its central tenets came from classical decision theory, including rationality, equilibrium or risk-free arbitrage, and efficient markets with "fair" pricing. Statman (1999, p. 19) asserts, "Standard finance is compelling because it uses a minimum of tools to build a unified theory intended to answer all the questions of finance."

According to Barberis and Thaler (2003, p. 1055), this framework is "appealingly simple" but has difficulty explaining individual and market behavior. Modern finance offered the dominant paradigms taught by finance academics and adopted by mainstream finance practitioners through the early 2000s. Many consider Eugene F. Fama, a 2013 Nobel laureate in economic sciences, the "father of modern finance."

According to Statman (2017), standard finance has five building blocks.

1. People are rational.
2. People construct portfolios as described by mean-variance portfolio theory.
3. People save and spend as described by standard life-cycle theory.
4. Standard asset pricing theory accounts for an investment's expected returns, where differences in risk determine differences in expected returns.
5. Markets are efficient.

Standard finance assumes people are rational and fully informed. They are immune to cognitive, emotional, and social errors in processing and responding to information when pursuing practical benefits. These self-interested decision-makers evaluate all outcomes under conditions of uncertainty to identify the best or optimal decision. In theory, rational utility maximizers determine the optimal choice by selecting the highest expected utility. In economics, *utility* is the usefulness or enjoyment of consuming a good or service. Calculating expected utility involves evaluating the utility for each outcome and weighting the assigned number by the outcome probability. In simpler terms, people analyze the pros and cons of any situation and then select the best one for them.

Mean-variance portfolio theory is a mathematical framework for constructing an asset portfolio to maximize the expected return for a given risk level. This theory traces back to Markowitz (1952). An investor measures an asset's risk based on a statistical measure called variance and then compares that measure with an asset's expected return (i.e., the mean). *Variance* is the average of the squared differences from the mean. Mean-variance optimization aims to maximize an investment's reward based on its risk. In other words, an investor can optimize a portfolio's expected returns for the desired risk level through diversification. *Diversification* combines different assets within a portfolio to smooth out *unsystematic risk*, the risk specific to investing in a particular investment that does not affect all securities in a market. This strategy seeks to combine assets in a portfolio with returns that are not perfectly positively correlated to lower portfolio risk without sacrificing expected return. Thus, diversification balances the negative performance of a given investment with the positive performance of different investments within a portfolio. In practice, the standard deviation is the most widely used measure of risk because it uses the original units of the data, not squared units as with the variance, making interpretation easier.

The *life-cycle hypothesis* (LCH) is an economic theory describing someone's spending and saving habits over a lifetime. According to this theory, individuals strive to smooth consumption during their lifetime – borrowing in low-income periods and saving during high-income periods. The LCH predicts wealth accumulation follows a hump-shaped curve – the savings rate is low when young, high during middle age, and low when old (Horton, 2021). It also implies that younger people can take more significant investment risks than more senior individuals who need to draw down accumulated savings. Modigliani and Brumberg (1954) developed a spending theory assuming that people make intelligent choices about how much they want to spend at each age, limited only by the resources available over their lives.

Standard asset pricing theory suggests that a particular asset's expected return depends only on the non-diversifiable portion of its total risk, called *systematic risk*. Classical decision theory focuses on risk and expected return. It assumes that rational people are risk-averse regarding their wealth and have consistent preferences, even in complex situations (Ackert, 2014). According to *The Economic Times* (2021), a risk-averse investor prefers lower returns with known risks rather than higher returns with unknown risks. Thus, if investments have the same return with different levels of risk, an investor should always prefer the investment with the lowest risk. People also expect higher returns to compensate them for taking more perceived risks. Standard finance theory views risk as an objective term that is quantifiable, often measured by standard deviation or beta. *Beta* measures a security or portfolio's volatility or systematic risk relative to the market. It assumes a linear relationship between risk and return. Thus, if perceived risk increases, so will the expected return.

Early asset pricing models focused on equilibrium pricing for equities, where macroeconomic variables determine prices. For example, the capital asset pricing model (CAPM) assumes the variable is the overall market and uses beta as its risk measure. Over time, numerous asset pricing models have emerged for equities and other asset classes. For example, Fama and French (1993) expanded on the CAPM by adding size and value factors to the market risk factor. Carhart (1997) created a four-factor model by extending the Fama–French model to contain an additional momentum factor. Fama and French (2015) enhanced their three-factor model by adding profitability and investment.

Finally, standard finance views markets as efficient and firms as rational wealth-maximizing organizations. An *efficient market* is one in which security prices reflect all relevant information (Fama, 1970). Evidence supporting the efficient market hypothesis (EMH) implies that an average investor cannot consistently beat the market, and the market knows best.

Over time, contributions in modern finance grew to include such ground-breaking paradigms as modern portfolio theory (MPT) or portfolio optimization (Markowitz, 1952, 1959), irrelevance theorems (Modigliani and Miller, 1958; Miller and Modigliani, 1961), asset pricing models such as the capital asset pricing model (CAPM) (Treynor, 1962; Sharpe, 1964; Lintner, 1965a, 1965b; Mossin, 1966), arbitrage pricing theory (APT) (Ross, 1976), the efficient market hypothesis (EMH) (Fama, 1965; Samuelson, 1965), and the option pricing model (Black and Scholes, 1973; Merton, 1973). Various finance pioneers won the Nobel Prize, including Fama, Markowitz, Merton, Miller, Modigliani, Samuelson, and Sharpe. Although their theories and models are elegant, they often offer low explanatory or predictive power (Haugen, 2002).

Behavioral finance

Although early attempts to bring psychology into finance date back to the 1920s and 1930s, "modern" behavioral finance gained considerable traction when the foundation of modern finance began to weaken as mounting evidence of irrational behavior and inefficient markets emerged, especially in the 1980s and 1990s. Conventional finance theory describes how people and markets should behave in "idealized" situations. It tries to explain the actions of the perfect "economic or rational man" (*Homo economicus*). However, its assumptions oversimply reality. Bloomfield (2010, p. 23) comments, "Anyone with a spouse, child, boss, or modicum of self-insight knows that the assumption of *Homo economicus* is false." Behavioral finance seeks to replace oversimplistic assumptions with a more realistic view of financial actors.

Behavioral finance sheds light on actual financial behavior. Szyszka (2010, p. 351) notes, "Any theory is only as good as its ability to explain or predict the processes actually taking place." Ackert (2014, p. 39) concludes, "Observation of actual behavior informs the development of good theory." Behavioral finance offers a new paradigm. However, Bloomfield (2010, p. 26) states, "New paradigms become successful only if they can explain anomalies of sufficient quantity and importance in a sufficiently simple way."

The new finance – behavioral finance – offers an alternative view that has revolutionized notions about how people and markets behave (Byrne and Brooks, 2008). It accounts for real-world anomalies and behaviors and why people make financial decisions. Thus, traditional finance is normative and behavioral finance is positive. A problem with standard finance is that it holds people and markets to too high a standard. This problem stems from its underlying assumptions. Behavioral finance has different fundamental beliefs and views people as human, not perfectly rational. Therefore, their risk attitudes and behaviors frequently diverge from the premise of optimal behavior patterns in traditional finance theories.

According to Byrne and Brooks (2008, p. 2), "the existing academic literature has tended to develop behavioral finance against the 'foil' of traditional rational finance." Thus, behavioral finance counters each assumption of standard finance. For example, it faults economic and financial models for assuming people are rational. People are not machines; they're fallible. They do not always make sound decisions or have complete information. Instead, people analyze data through the lenses of their experience, knowledge, and biases. If they were always rational and markets were efficient, the world would be more straightforward. However, people and markets are complex. Behavioral finance assumes that people are sometimes irrational and make inconsistent financial decisions, and that markets are not always efficient. Human

biases, emotions, and cognitive limitations in processing and responding to information affect economic behavior. According to Ibbotson et
al. (2018), researchers have accumulated much evidence that investors
are not entirely rational and are far from fully informed. Consequently,
they make all kinds of foolish decisions. Thus, behavioral finance offers
a guide to improving financial decisions by understanding how and when
people and markets deviate from the restrictive assumptions of standard
finance.

Early researchers in behavioral finance homed in on "shooting arrows
into the soft spots of standard finance, especially in the 1980s" (Statman,
1999, p. 18). During that period, researchers often focused on explaining
various anomalies, biases, and heuristics in financial markets. However,
behaviorists point out that irrational behavior is commonplace rather
than an anomaly. Market efficiency was at the center of the battle between
standard and behavioral finance. This research was critical of the standard
finance assumptions. It showed how people's behavior deviated from
traditional economic models in predictable ways.

Early behavioral finance theory

Early behavioral finance theory rests on cognitive psychology, limits to
arbitrage, and investor sentiment.

Cognitive psychology

Many consider Israeli psychologists Daniel Kahneman and Amos Tversky
the fathers of behavioral finance. Their collaborations started in the late
1960s, resulting in works whose psychological concepts have implications
for behavioral finance. Kahneman was the first psychologist to win the
Nobel Memorial Prize in Economic Sciences in 2002. The introduction of
the CAPM and the EMH was a catalyst for Tversky and Kahneman (1974)
to start questioning the assumption that investors behave as rational
agents (Kahneman and Tversky, 1979).

Other relevant contributors to behavioral finance beginning in the 1970s
and 1980s were Hersh Shefrin and Meir Statman. For example, they introduced the term "behavioral finance" at the first-ever American Finance

Association session in behavioral finance in 1984. A "breakthrough" in the emergence of "modern" behavioral finance was the paper by Shefrin and Statman (1984), providing a behavioral explanation for why Miller and Modigliani's (1961) irrelevance theory does not apply to dividends. It was the first academic paper in behavioral finance to apply Kahneman and Tversky's prospect theory, discussed later in this chapter.

Shefrin and Statman contributed numerous books about behavioral finance. For example, Shefrin's (1999) *Beyond Greed and Fear* was the first comprehensive book on behavioral finance. Other notable works focus on behavioral aspects of corporate finance (Shefrin, 2001b, 2006), asset pricing (Shefrin, 2005), and risk management (Shefrin, 2016). Statman (2010, 2017, 2019) sought to understand how investors and managers make financial decisions and how financial markets reflect these decisions.

Another major contributor is Richard Thaler, who received the 2017 Nobel Memorial Prize in Economic Sciences for his contributions to behavioral economics. He combined economics, finance, and psychology to develop concepts like mental accounting (Thaler, 1985, 1999), the endowment effect (Kahneman et al., 1990), and other biases affecting behavior (Kahneman et al., 1991; Benartzi and Thaler, 1995). Thaler and Sunstein (2008) popularized the concept of the *nudge*, a conceptual device for leading people to make better decisions. They describe a situation involving nudges as *libertarian paternalism*: libertarian because it enables choice, but paternalistic because it fosters specific behavior. Chapter 7 provides a detailed discussion of nudging.

Limits to arbitrage

Another essential component of behavioral finance relates to the limits to arbitrage. Few defenders of the EMH believed that all investors make decisions according to the rational axioms of choice under uncertainty. Instead, they thought efficient markets could exist when some irrational investors make systematic errors if rational investors (arbitrageurs) intervened to bring prices to their intrinsic values. They do this through arbitrage, buying cheap assets and selling expensive ones. This logic suggests that market prices will still be rational. Although arbitrage exists due to market inefficiencies, it exploits and resolves them. However, behavioral finance theory maintains that this argument is flawed because arbitrage is risky and costly, limiting the arbitrageurs' demand for fair-value restoring trades (Shleifer and Vishny, 1997). Thus, the limits to arbitrage result from restrictions on funds that rational traders use to arbitrage away pricing inefficiencies, permitting prices to diverge from an asset's intrinsic value, even with rational arbitrageurs.

According to Wei and Zhang (2006), three risk categories result in the limits of arbitrage: (1) fundamental risk, (2) noise trader risk, and (3) implementation risk. *Fundamental risk* is the risk that arbitrageurs may be incorrect about the basic values of their positions. *Noise trader risk* is a type of market risk associated with the investment decisions of uninformed, emotional, and undisciplined traders, leading to mispricing. Well-disciplined and knowledgeable traders can lose money due to excess market noise. Arbitrageurs still try to exploit the mispricing that could worsen in the short run. *Implementation risk* arises when transaction costs or short-sale constraints completely erode arbitrage returns. Thus, prices may diverge from intrinsic value and remain in non-equilibrium for protracted periods. Despite early support for the EMH, numerous theoretical and empirical challenges to it emerged, revealing that market efficiency is a special case under some implausible assumptions (Shleifer, 2000; Haugen, 2002).

Investor sentiment

The standard finance model forces capital market prices to equal the present value of expected future cash flows while incorporating the risk of those cash flows. Markets remain efficient, assuming unlimited arbitrage and no irrational disturbances (i.e., investor sentiment). *Investor sentiment* is a belief about future cash flows and investment risks not justified by the facts (Baker and Wurgler, 2007). It concerns how real-world investors form their beliefs, valuations, and demands for securities (Schleifer, 2000). However, investment sentiment plays little role in asset pricing in traditional finance theory.

In behavioral finance, investors' general outlook or attitude toward a particular security or the overall financial market is essential because it drives demand and supply, resulting in price movements. Thus, investor sentiment affects asset prices and markets. Evidence suggests that investor sentiment affects stock returns, especially for stocks that are difficult to value or arbitrage (Baker and Wurgler, 2006; Kumar and Lee, 2006; Tetlock, 2007). Chapter 6 discusses how social interaction generates sentiment.

Investor sentiment can lead to optimism or pessimism, where disparities between prices and values are significant and persist for months or years. For example, with a positive asset bubble, market participants drive an asset's price above its value relative to some stock valuation system. Examples include the dot-com bubble (2000), housing bubble (2005), oil asset bubble (2008), gold asset bubble (2011), Treasury notes bubble (2012), stock market bubble (2013), and bitcoin asset bubble (2017).

Central theories and tenets of behavioral finance

Various foundational theories and principles emerged during behavioral finance's first several decades. These new ways of thinking arose because the traditional finance paradigm could not adequately explain observed financial behavior. This section reviews some theoretical and conceptual underpinnings of behavioral finance.

Behavioral decision theory and bounded rationality

Rationality is the idea that people always choose the most optimal decision when serving their self-interest. Behavioral decision theory postulates various forms of psychologically grounded investor "irrationality." Simon (1957), a Nobel laureate, proposed the concept of "bounded rationality" to replace the perfect rationality assumptions of *homo economicus* with those consistent with cognitively limited individuals. Bounded rationality addresses flaws in the original rational choice theory by highlighting limitations in making optimal decisions. *Bounded rationality* is the notion that people have limited cognitive ability, information, and time and do not always make the "correct" choice, despite the availability of data pointing them toward a particular course of action. Additionally, their perceptions or other investors' decisions may guide their decisions, not fundamental rules. Therefore, individuals reduce their options and data collection to simplify the decision.

According to behavioral decision theory, a person makes a satisfactory but not necessarily optimal choice. In other words, a decision choice is often good enough rather than the best possible. For example, suppose you want to replace your cell phone by the end of the month but do not know which is best for you. You face many choices, limited information on each product, and a time constraint. Because these three factors create boundaries that limit your ability to choose, you settle for the most popular phone in your price range. Therefore, bounded rationality implies that you exhibit "Normal behavior" when making decisions. As Baker et al. (2005, p. 257) note, "normal behavior is what people really do as opposed to what they should do according to the economic definition of a rational person."

Prospect theory and loss aversion

Behavioral finance challenges using conventional utility functions based on risk aversion, namely *subjective expected utility* (SEU) *theory*. SEU theory assumes people choose an outcome that provides maximum utility given the probability of outcomes. It also holds that they are concerned with their long-run state of wealth and do not attach different weights to losses and gains in wealth. As an alternative to SEU theory, Kahneman and Tversky (1979) propose *prospect theory* (PT), also called *loss aversion theory*, a descriptive theory of decision-making that describes how people behave when given choices involving probability. PT recognizes that people may make a choice that does not necessarily maximize utility because they rank other considerations above utility. It assumes that changes in wealth and the subjective value of such changes often determine choice behavior. Kahneman and Tversky contend that people evaluate outcomes against a subjective reference point, such as the status quo or an asset's purchase price. PT provides the first theoretical foundation of behavioral finance and casts doubt on the validity of many theoretical models and evidence based on SEU. PT is among the most often used theoretical lenses in the literature because of its broad range of uses in various contexts.

According to PT, people value gains and losses differently. They are more concerned about losing what they have and less about profits. That is, individuals attach greater weight to losses than to equivalent gains in wealth (Altman, 2010). Tversky and Kahneman's (1992) research shows that losses are twice as consequential as the same gains. PT's value function curve is S-shaped: convex for "gains" and concave for "losses." It is much steeper to the left of the reference point when the "loss" is small than to the right of that point when the "gain" is small. Thus, the S-shaped curve indicates that people are generally risk-averse in the domain of gains and risk-seeking in the domain of losses. Losses outweigh gains because the value function is asymmetric and steeper for losses than gains.

PT asserts that people are *loss-averse*, meaning that the negative emotional impact of a loss exceeds the positive effects of the same amount of gain when assessing financial transactions. For example, losing a $100 bill might be more painful than finding a $100 would be joyful. Because people are more sensitive to losses than gains, they try to avoid losses. PT can explain why people exhibit risk-seeking behavior when facing losses, especially when trying to get back to even, and risk-averse behavior when facing gains. Loss aversion also helps to keep the status quo because people hate the feeling of regret and are less motivated by gains of the same size.

Kahneman and Tversky (1979) consider PT different and superior to Simon's (1957) bounded rationality approach. They contend that key factors explaining human choice behavior are emotive variables, generating choice behavior inconsistent with SEU theory. According to (Altman, 2010, p. 197), "Prospect theory is the foundation for a variety of descriptive propositions pertaining to so-called persistent biased decision making under risk and uncertainty." By contrast, Simon focuses more on the human brain's limited capacity to process information and the features of the information that require processing.

Pan (2019) identifies PT's four main contributions.

- People value the absolute amount of wealth and the change in wealth. Thus, investors are more concerned about an investment's profit or loss than its total amount.
- People are more inclined to take risks when facing the prospect of loss with similar conditions (risk preference) but are more prone to achieve sure profits when facing the prospect of profit with similar conditions (risk aversion).
- The pain of a decrease in wealth is greater than the pleasure of increasing wealth by the same amount.
- An early decision's results affect the later risk attitude and decision. Early profits can enhance people's risk preference and smooth the later losses, while early losses exacerbate the pain of later losses and increase risk aversion.

Cumulative prospect theory

Prospect theory continued to develop from the 1980s onward. A breakthrough occurred with Tversky and Kahneman's (1992) cumulative prospect theory (CPT), a modified version of PT. CPT differs from PT in that weighting is applied to the cumulative probability distribution function, as in rank-dependent SEU, but not to individual outcomes' probabilities. People make choices based on changes in wealth rather than total wealth. An S-shape value function characterizes the decision weights. Although Levy (2010) notes that dozens of studies verify CPT, his tests are less supportive but do not invalidate CPT. In summary, PT and CPT are cornerstones in the behavioral finance paradigm and offer better descriptions of choice behavior than conventional models, like SEU.

The disposition effect

One of the most studied investing patterns is an anomaly discovered in behavioral finance called the disposition effect (Zhu, 2010). First uncovered by Shefrin and Statman (1985), the *disposition effect* refers to the tendency of investors to sell winning investments (winners) too quickly and to hold on to losing investments (losers) too long. One explanation for the disposition effect is emotions. Investors dislike the experience of loss, so they irrationally refuse to accept it. This nonstandard investor preference is inconsistent with the axioms of expected utility theory and hence difficult to explain rationally. This bias harms wealth because it can increase capital gains taxes or reduce investment returns even before taxes.

Kaustia (2010a) reviews the empirical evidence on the disposition effect in trading behavior. His analysis shows that the disposition effect varies by investor type, with retail (individual) investors more affected than professional investors. Shefrin and Statman (1985) consider the potential underlying causes of the disposition effect using PT, mental accounting, regret aversion, and self-control. They conclude that the reason is psychological. However, later research suggests that PT cannot easily generate the disposition effect (Barberis and Xiong, 2009; Kaustia, 2010b).

A reduction in the disposition effect can be achieved through *hedonic framing*, a mental strategy to maximize the positive impact of gains and minimize the adverse effects of losses. Thus, it describes how people try to maximize psychological pleasure and minimize pain when facing decisions involving gains and losses. Hedonic framing forces individuals to treat gains and losses differently. Thaler (1985) suggests four strategies.

- *Separate gains.* Think of a single large gain as several smaller gains. In PT, the gain function is concave, suggesting that people experience diminishing sensitivity to incremental increases. Thus, five gains of $1,000 each feel better than one gain of $5,000. Consequently, maximizing the hedonic impact of gains involves spreading the gains across separate periods, not aggregating them into a single event.
- *Combine losses.* Think of several minor losses as a single large loss. In PT, the loss function is convex, indicating that people experience diminishing sensitivity to losses. A single loss of $5,000 does not feel as bad as five losses of $1,000. Thus, minimizing the hedonic impact of losses involves aggregating the losses into one episode.
- *Combine smaller losses with larger gains.* Think of a major gain and a minor loss as a net minor gain. In PT, the value function is steeper for losses than for gains, resulting in loss aversion. The interaction of loss aversion with diminishing sensitivity for gains suggests the benefits of integrating a large gain with smaller losses to counteract disproportionate disutility from losses. People feel better getting a single gain of $4,000 than a gain of $5,000 paired with a loss of $1,000.
- *Separate smaller gains from larger losses.* Consider the two separately in the case of a major loss and a minor gain. Because the value function for gains is concave and steepest near the origin, people should try to experience as many small gains as possible. People feel better with a small gain of $50 on one day with an unrelated loss of $1,000 the following day than a single combined loss of $950 (Cohen, 2016).

These strategies emphasize the positive and trick the brain into thinking that more good things happen than bad. These approaches can assist in controlling emotions and improving decision-making.

Mental accounting

Thaler (1980, 1985, 1999) and Tversky and Kahneman (1981) developed the concept of mental accounting. Thaler (1999, p. 183) defines mental accounting as "the set of cognitive operations used by individuals and households to organize, evaluate, and keep track of financial activities." In other words, people categorize or group money into different mental "buckets" and decide how to use the funds based on these buckets. According to mental accounting, people think about money depending on the circumstances, such as its source or intended use. This psychological phenomenon results in dividing transactions into separate accounts and treating payoffs differently across these accounts, despite money being fungible.

Mental accounts offer potential benefits and drawbacks. On the positive side, mental accounts can help people keep track of their money and direct it to where they want it. For example, mentally assigning some cash as an emergency fund could help prevent spending these funds for other purposes. Mental accounts can also serve as a self-control strategy and facilitate savings for larger purposes. As Baker and Ricciardi (2015) note, treating certain mental accounts, such as saving for a college education, as long-term investments may help people reach their financial goals.

Yet mental accounting can prompt biases and systematic departures from choices that are rational or ideal. Mental accounting causes investors to view each investment separately, minimizing their view of portfolio diversification. Here are several other examples of mental accounting. Investors may consider unrealized gains and losses less significant than realized ones. These investors may view profits as not mattering until they close a position. Another example of mental accounting is separating purchases into cash and credit card purchases. People are generally more willing to pay for goods using credit cards than cash.

A third example is treating credit card rewards as "other money." Parting with it is easier than parting with "earned money." A final but similar example is keeping the capital or principal in a separate mental account from the profits from selling a stock. Consequently, investors may take greater risks with the gains because they view them as "playing with house money." This gambling term indicates that they "won" money from the house, which is the stock market here. Viewing capital gains as "free money" that these investors can afford to lose is a mental creation. As Baker and Puttonen (2019, p. 51) note, "This psychological phenomenon is economically irrational because money is money regardless of its origin or intended use. A dollar in your right pocket is worth the same as one in your left pocket."

Framing

Framing refers to how someone describes the setting for a decision or presents information. In traditional finance, framing shouldn't influence decisions because rational decision-makers should see through the frame. They focus on the information, not its presentation. However, different presentations of information can lead to varying judgments and decisions. The *framing effect* is the tendency to behave differently depending on the presentation of information. It is a factor if someone can't see how someone presents data to them. As Yazdipour and Howard (2010, p. 44) note, "Framing effects are other key psychological facts that seriously call into question traditional theory's rationality assumptions."

Tversky and Kahneman (1981) confirm the framing effect's legitimacy in influencing choices. They show that phrasing the same decision problem in terms of gains or losses may alter someone's choice. People tend to choose the option that appears as a gain, not a loss. For example, investment A increased in value by $500 during a given year. Investment B initially increased in value by a $1,000 gain but declined by $500 near year-end due to market volatility. Both options result in a $500 gain but have different frames. What investment is preferable? If people were perfectly rational, their answers should be the same. Yet they favor the first option because it does not present a loss. People prefer something presented positively or in a context that offers benefits than presented with a negative frame. For example, someone may unwisely choose a high-risk investment portfolio because an advisor emphasized the upside instead of the potential downside.

A frame's size is also relevant. *Narrow framing* refers to people viewing each share or investment in isolation. The frame of reference is the individual company or investment. Those engaged in narrow framing can't see the "big picture." They tend to see investments without considering the context of their overall portfolio or wealth, which would involve using a wider frame. Investors who make decisions based on a narrow frame of reference focus on short-term losses. They also have poorly diversified portfolios compared to investors using wider frames, resulting in more volatility and higher risk. Another term for framing is choice architecture, discussed in more detail in Chapter 7.

Summary and conclusions

Standard finance assumes that people are rational actors and self-interested utility maximizers, free from biases. It also holds that markets are efficient. Behavioral finance counters each of these assumptions. Although the assumptions, concepts, and theories underlying standard and behavioral finance seem mutually exclusive, they're complementary. Both academic schools of thought provide valuable contributions and are not an "either-or" proposition. By understanding how and when people deviate from rational expectations, behavioral finance offers a blueprint for making better financial decisions. However, blending both approaches will likely to improve understanding and the ability to engage in better decision-making.

References

Ackert, Lucy F. 2014. "Traditional and Behavioral Finance." In H. Kent Baker and Victor Ricciardi (eds.), *Investor Behavior: The Psychology of Financial Planning and Investing*, 25–41. Hoboken, NJ: John Wiley & Sons, Inc.

Altman, Morris. 2010. "Prospect Theory and Behavioral Finance." In H. Kent Baker and John R. Nofsinger (eds.), *Behavioral Finance: Investors, Corporations, and Market*, 191–209. Hoboken, NJ: John Wiley & Sons, Inc.

Baker, August J., Dennis E. Logue, and Jack S. Rader. 2005. *Managing Pension and Retirement Plans: A Guide for Employers, Administrators, and Other Fiduciaries*. New York: Oxford University Press.

Baker, H. Kent, and Vesa Puttonen. 2019. *Navigating the Investment Minefield: A Practical Guide to Avoiding Mistakes, Biases, and Traps*. Bingley, UK: Emerald Publishing Limited.

Baker, H. Kent, and Victor Ricciardi. 2015. "Understanding Behavioral Aspects of Financial Planning and Investing." *Journal of Financial Planning* 28:3, 22–26.

Baker, Malcolm, and Jeffrey Wurgler. 2006. "Investor Sentiment and the Cross-Section of Stock Returns." *Journal of Finance* 61:4, 1645–1680.

Baker, Malcolm, and Jeffrey Wurgler. 2007. "Investor Sentiment in the Stock Market." *Journal of Economic Perspectives* 21:2, 129–151.

Barberis, Nicholas, and Richard H. Thaler. 2003. "A Survey of Behavioral Finance." In George M. Constantinides, Milton Harris, and René M. Stulz (eds.), *Handbook of the Economics of Finance*, 1053–1128. Amsterdam: North-Holland.

Barberis, Nicholas, and Wei Xiong. 2009. "What Drives the Disposition Effect? An Analysis of a Long-Standing Preference-Based Explanation." *Journal of Finance* 64:2, 751–784.

Benartzi, Shlomo, and Richard H. Thaler. 1995. "Myopic Loss Aversion and the Equity Premium Puzzle." *Quarterly Journal of Economics* 110:1, 73–92.

Black, Fischer, and Myron Scholes. 1973. "The Pricing of Options and Corporate Liabilities." *Journal of Political Economy* 81:3, 637–654.

Bloomfield, Robert. 2010. "Traditional versus Behavioral Finance." In H. Kent Baker and John R. Nofsinger (eds.), *Behavioral Finance: Investors, Corporations, and Market*, 23–38. Hoboken, NJ: John Wiley & Sons, Inc.

Byrne, Alistair, and Mike Brooks. 2008. *Behavioral Finance: Theories and Evidence.* Charlottesville, VA: The Research Foundation of CFA Institute.

Carhart, Michael M. 1997. "On Persistence in Mutual Fund Performance." *Journal of Finance* 52:1: 57–82.

Cohen, Paul M. 2016. "Three Rules from Prospect Theory on Experience Design." January 19. Available at https://paulcohen.com/lessons-from-prospect-theory-on-experience-design/.

Crosby, Daniel. 2014. "Investor Emotions and Financial Decisions." In Chuck Widger and Daniel Crosby (eds.), *Personal Benchmark: Integrating Behavioral Finance and Investment Management*, 49–82. Hoboken, NJ: John Wiley & Sons, Inc.

Fama, Eugene F. 1965. "The Behavior of Stock-Market Prices." *Journal of Business* 38:1, 34– 105.

Fama, Eugene F. 1970. "Efficient Capital Markets: A Review of Theory and Empirical Work." *Journal of Finance* 25:2, 383–417.

Fama, Eugene F., and Kenneth R. French. 1993. "Common Risk Factors in the Returns on Stocks and Bonds." *Journal of Financial Economics* 33:1, 3–56.

Fama, Eugene F., and Kenneth R. French. 2015. "A Five-Factor Asset Pricing Model." *Journal of Financial Economics* 116:1, 1–22.

Haugen, Robert A. 2002. *The Inefficient Stock Market: What Pays Off and Why*, Second Edition. Upper Saddle River, NJ: Pearson Education Inc.

Hayes, Adam. 2021. "Finance." *Investopedia*, July 10. Available at https://www.investopedia.com/terms/f/finance.asp#:~:text=The%20history%20of%20finance%20and,as%20early%20as%201000%20BC.

Horton, Cassidy. 2021. "What Is the Life-Cycle Hypothesis?" *The Balance*, December 31. Available at https://www.thebalance.com/what-is-the-life-cycle-hypothesis-5209285.

Ibbotson, Roger G., Thomas M. Idzorek, Paul D. Kaplan, and James X. Xiong. 2018. *Popularity: A Bridge between Classical and Behavioral Finance.* Charlottesville, VA: CFA Institute Research Foundation.

Kahneman, Daniel, Jack L. Knetsch, and Richard H. Thaler. 1990. "Experimental Tests of the Endowment Effect and the Coase Theorem." *Journal of Political Economy* 98:6. 1325–1348.

Kahneman, Daniel, Jack L. Knetsch, and Richard H. Thaler. 1991. "Anomalies: The Endowment Effect, Loss Aversion, and Status Quo Bias." *Journal of Economic Perspectives* 5:1, 193–206.

Kahneman, Daniel, and Amos Tversky. 1979. "Prospect Theory: An Analysis of Decision under Risk." *Econometrica* 47:2, 263–191.

Kaustia, Markku. 2010a. "Disposition Effect." In H. Kent Baker and John R. Nofsinger (eds.), *Behavioral Finance: Investors, Corporations, and Market*, 171–189. Hoboken, NJ: John Wiley & Sons, Inc.

Kaustia, Markku. 2010b. "Prospect Theory and the Disposition Effect." *Journal of Financial and Quantitative Analysis* 45:3, 791–812.
Kumar, Alok, and Charles M. C. Lee. 2006. "Retail Investor Sentiment and Return Comovements." *Journal of Finance* 61:5, 2451–2486.
Levy, Hail. 2010. "Cumulative Prospect Theory: Tests Using the Stochastic Dominance Approach." In H. Kent Baker and John R. Nofsinger (eds.), *Behavioral Finance: Investors, Corporations, and Market*, 211–239. Hoboken, NJ: John Wiley & Sons, Inc.
Lintner, John. 1965a. "The Valuation of Risk Assets and the Selection of Risky Investments in Stock Portfolios and Capital Budgets." *Review of Economics and Statistics* 47:1, 13–37.
Lintner, John. 1965b. "Security Prices, Risk and Maximal Gains from Diversification." *Journal of Finance* 20:4, 587–615.
Markowitz, Harry. 1952. "Portfolio Selection." *Journal of Finance* 7:1, 77–91.
Markowitz, Harry. 1959. *Portfolio Selection: Efficient Diversifications of Investments.* Cowles Foundation Monograph No. 16. New York: John Wiley & Sons, Inc.
Merton, Robert C. 1973. "Theory of Rational Option Pricing." *Bell Journal of Economics and Management Science* 4:1, 141–183.
Miller, Merton H., and Franco Modigliani. 1961. "Dividend Policy, Growth, and the Valuation of Shares." *Journal of Business* 34:4, 411–433.
Modigliani, Franco, and Richard Brumberg. 1954. "Utility Analysis and the Consumption Function: An Interpretation of Cross-Section Data." Kenneth Kurihara (ed.), *Post Keynesian Economics*, 388–436. New Brunswick, NJ: Rutgers University Press.
Modigliani, Franco, and Merton H. Miller. 1958. "The Cost of Capital, Corporation Finance and the Theory of Investment." *American Economic Review* 48:3, 261–297.
Mossin, Jan. 1966. "Equilibrium in a Capital Asset Market." *Econometrica* 34:4, 768–873.
Pan, Ze. 2019. "A Review of Prospect Theory." *Journal of Human Resource and Sustainability Studies* 7:1, 98–107.
Ross, Stephen A. 1976. "Arbitrage Theory of Capital Asset Pricing." *Journal of Economic Theory* 13:1, 341–360.
Samuelson, Paul A. 1965. "Rational Theory of Warrant Pricing." *Industrial Management Review* 6:2, 13–39.
Sharpe, William F. 1964. "Capital Asset Prices: A Theory of Market Equilibrium under Conditions of Risk." *Journal of Finance* 19:3, 425–442.
Shefrin, Hersh. 1999. *Beyond Greed and Fear: Understanding Behavioral Finance and the Psychology of Investing.* Boston, MA: Harvard Business School Press.
Shefrin, Hersh. 2001a. *Behavioral Finance.* Cheltenham, U.K. and Northampton, MA, U.S.A.: Edward Elgar Publishing.
Shefrin, Hersh. 2001b. "Behavioral Corporate Finance." *Journal of Applied Corporate Finance* 14:3, 113–126.
Shefrin, Hersh. 2005. *A Behavioral Approach to Asset Pricing.* Amsterdam: Academic Press.
Shefrin, Hersh. 2006. *Behavioral Corporate Finance.* New York: McGraw-Hill/Irwin.

Shefrin, Hersh. 2016. *Behavioral Risk Management: Managing the Psychology that Drives Decisions and Influences Operational Risk*. New York: Palgrave Macmillan.

Shefrin, Hersh, and Meir Statman. 1984. "Explaining Investor Preference for Cash Dividends." *Journal of Financial Economics* 13:2, 253–282.

Shefrin, Hersh, and Meir Statman. 1985. "The Disposition to Sell Winners Too Early and Ride Losers Too Long." *Journal of Finance* 40:3, Papers and Proceedings of the Forty-Third Annual Meeting American Finance Association, Dallas, Texas, December 28–30, 1984, 777–790.

Shiller, Robert J. 2003. "From Efficient Markets Theory to Behavioral Finance." *Journal of Economic Perspectives* 17:1, 83–104.

Shleifer, Andrei. 2000. *Inefficient Markets: An Introduction to Behavioral Finance*. New York: Oxford University Press.

Shleifer, Andrei., and Robert W. Vishny. 1997. "The Limits of Arbitrage." *Journal of Finance* 52:1, 35–55.

Simon, Herbert A. 1957. *Models of Man*. New York: John Wiley & Sons, Inc.

Simpson, Stephen D. 2021. "Finance vs. Economics: What's the Difference?" *Investopedia*, June 23. Available at https://www.investopedia.com/articles/economics/11/difference-between-finance-and-economics.asp.

Statman, Meir. 1999. "Behavioral Finance: Past Battles and Future Engagements." *Financial Analysts Journal* 55:6, 18–27.

Statman, Meir. 2010. *What Investors Really Want: Know What Drives Investor Behavior and Make Smarter Financial Decisions*. New York: McGraw-Hill.

Statman, Meir. 2017. *Finance for Normal People: How Investors and Markets Behave*. New York: Oxford University Press.

Statman, Meir. 2019. *Behavioral Finance: The Second Generation*. Charlottesville, VA: CFA Institute Research Foundation.

Szyszka, Adam. 2010. "Belief- and Preference-Bases Models." In H. Kent Baker and John R. Nofsinger (eds.), *Behavioral Finance: Investors, Corporations, and Markets*, 351–372. Hoboken, NJ: John Wiley & Sons, Inc.

Tetlock, Paul C. 2007. "Giving Content to Investor Sentiment: The Role of Media in the Stock Market." *Journal of Finance* 62:3, 1139–1168.

Thaler, Richard H. 1980. "Toward a Positive Theory of Consumer Choice." *Journal of Economic Behavior and Organization* 1:1, 39–60.

Thaler, Richard H. 1985. "Mental Accounting and Consumer Choice." *Marketing Science* 4:3, 199–214.

Thaler, Richard H. 1999. "Mental Accounting Matters." *Journal of Behavioral Decision Making* 12:3: 183–206.

Thaler, Richard H. 2015. *Misbehaving: The Making of Behavioral Economics*. New York and London: W. W. Norton & Company.

Thaler, Richard H., and Cass R. Sunstein. 2008. *Nudge: Improving Decisions about Health, Wealth, and Happiness*. New Haven, CT: Yale University Press.

The Economic Times. 2021. "Definition of 'Risk Averse,'" September 23. Available at https://economictimes.indiatimes.com/definition/risk-averse.

Treynor, Jack L. 1962. "Toward a Theory of Market Value of Risky Assets." Unpublished manuscript. Final version in Robert A. Korajczyk (ed.). 1999. *Asset Pricing and Portfolio Performance*, 15–22. London: Risk Books.

Tversky, Amos, and Daniel Kahneman. 1974. "Judgement and Uncertainty: Heuristics and Biases." *Science* 185:4147, 1124–1131.

Tversky, Amos, and Daniel Kahneman. 1981. "The Framing of Decisions and the Psychology of Choice." *Science* 211:4481, 453–458.

Tversky, Amos, and Daniel Kahneman. 1992. "Advances in Prospect Theory: Cumulative Representation of Uncertainty." *Journal of Risk and Uncertainty* 5:4, 297–323.

Wei, Kuo-Chiang (John), and Jie Zhang. 2006. "The Limits of Arbitrage: Evidence from Fundamental Value-to-Price Trading Strategies." Working Paper. Available at https://ssrn.com/abstract=891379.

Yazdipour, Rassoul, and James A. Howard. 2010. "Behavioral Finance: Applications and Pedagogy in Business Education and Training." In H. Kent Baker and John R. Nofsinger (eds.), *Behavioral Finance: Investors, Corporations, and Markets*, 39–56. Hoboken, NJ: John Wiley & Sons, Inc.

Zhu, Ning. 2010. "Individual Investor Trading." In H. Kent Baker and John R. Nofsinger (eds.), *Behavioral Finance: Investors, Corporations, and Markets*, 351–372. Hoboken, NJ: John Wiley & Sons, Inc.

2   Risk perspectives

Risk taking is any consciously, or non-consciously controlled behavior with a perceived uncertainty about its outcome, and/or about its possible benefits or costs for the physical, economic or psycho-social well-being of oneself or others.
–Rüdiger M. Trimpop (1994, p. 9)

Introduction

Whether investing in stocks or riding a roller coaster, individuals face risk and uncertainty. Some play games of chance, such as gambling. They hope for a large payoff but often lose their total bet. For example, purchasing a lottery ticket is a risky endeavor with a high probability of no gain and a minimal chance of a significant gain. Conversely, placing money in a savings account at a low fixed rate of return is a low-risk strategy because the person expects to earn a small gain for protecting the principal.

Risk is calculable, expected, and known. *Uncertainty* is immeasurable, unanticipated, and unknown. A judgment about risk occurs when probabilities with assigned future outcomes are accurately known, like poker statistics. A decision involving uncertainty occurs when an outcome's probabilities are not specifically known or understood, such as the results of political elections or sporting events. The main distinction between risk and uncertainty is that under risk a person can use statistical probabilities to assess potential results objectively whereas under uncertainty this is not the case.

This chapter explains why traditional risk measures, behavioral factors, and personal/demographical characteristics are the basis of individual risk perception and risk tolerance. It begins by discussing these two terms, followed by the importance of accounting data. The chapter then focuses on biases and issues influencing risk perception and risk tolerance before providing a summary and conclusions.

Risk perception

Risk perception is the subjective judgment process people apply when evaluating risk and uncertainty. It is the loss that an individual thinks might occur in purchasing a financial service or investment product, whether that actual risk exists or not. Perceived risk blends objective and subjective factors influencing how people make decisions about investment products and financial services. Ricciardi (2008a) identifies over 150 accounting and financial proxy variables, such as standard deviation and beta, from the risk perception literature as objective risk indicators. Risk's qualitative aspect is relevant for measuring, assessing, and describing risk. Ricciardi (2004, 2008b) also identifies more than 100 behavioral risk factors, like heuristics and worry, in the behavioral finance literature and over 10 subjective risk attributes in the behavioral accounting literature.

The relationship between risk and return

Standard finance assumes a positive relationship between risk and return. The basis of this connection is *risk aversion*, where people expect a higher return for investing in riskier securities, such as common stock. However, this positive link between risk and return does not always occur. Behavioral finance assumes a negative association between perceived risk and expected return (Ricciardi 2008a). For example, Shefrin's (2001) findings support an inverse relationship between perceived risk and expected return among students and experts when it comes to common stock. He suggests this result relates to the *representativeness heuristic*, which estimates an event's likelihood by comparing it to an existing prototype. Thus, people are inclined to have a predisposed belief about a financial product and then misjudge how much this product is like others. For instance, someone may see higher perceived returns with safe or quality stocks, like Apple, as having a lower perceived risk.

Risk tolerance

Risk tolerance is the amount of potential loss someone is willing to accept while making a judgment and decision about a financial security. Roszkowski and Davey (2010, p. 43) define risk tolerance as the "amount of risk that an individual is willing to accept in the pursuit of some goal."

Grable (2008, p. 4) describes risk tolerance as the "maximum amount of uncertainty someone is willing to accept when making a financial decision." In an interview, Geoff Davey described risk tolerance as a person's "psychological comfort with risk" (Schulaka, 2012, p. 17).

The Securities and Exchange Commission (2004, p. 2) provides the following comments on risk tolerance:

> What are the best saving and investing products for you? The answer depends on when you will need the money, your goals, and if you will be able to sleep at night if you purchase a risky investment where you could lose your principal.

The Securities and Exchange Commission (2010, p. 1) also views risk tolerance as "your ability and willingness to lose some or all of your original investment in exchange for greater potential returns."

Empirical findings on risk tolerance

The academic literature reports many findings about the differences in risk tolerance among people with varying demographic and socioeconomic characteristics. Grable (2008) reports the following general findings on how such characteristics affect risk-taking behavior.

- Age: Younger individuals are more risk aggressive than older people.
- Gender: Females are more risk-averse than males.
- Marital status: Single people make riskier judgments than married individuals.
- Education: Individuals with higher levels of education have an increased propensity to take risks compared to their less educated peers.

Link between risk perception and risk tolerance

The following researchers provide a connection between risk perception and risk tolerance. Martinussen and Hunter (2009, p. 198) assert that the two topics are "related and often confounded constructs." By contrast, Roszkowski and Davey (2010, p. 43) refer to research studies noting these two concepts "can independently contribute to risk-taking behavior." Littell et al. (2003, p. 248) propose that people "are often not fully aware of their true level of risk tolerance or of the factors that influence their perception of the riskiness of a situation." Financial professionals should understand the association between these two concepts of risk to ensure they develop an accurate risk profile and implement a sound investment strategy for their clients.

The significance of accounting data in risk perception studies

Investors often develop their risk perceptions for common stock based on accounting data and other financial statement information contained within the behavioral accounting literature. Hofstedt and Kinard (1970, p. 43) define *behavioral accounting* as "the study of the behavior of accountants or the behavior of non-accountants as they are influenced by accounting functions and reports. It cuts across financial, managerial, and tax accounting research." Behavioral accounting, with its literature containing concepts and theories such as risk-taking behavior, framing, heuristics, and prospect theory, has a shared research agenda with behavioral finance (Libby and Fishburn, 1977; Birnberg and Shields, 1989; Ashton and Ashton, 1999).

McDonald and Stehle's (1975) seminal research study in behavioral finance asked portfolio managers to rate their perceived risk of and familiarity with 25 stocks. The results reveal that beta and non-market risk explained 15 percent and 69 percent, respectively, of the variation in respondents' risk perception. Three variables explained 84 percent of the perceived risk for this stock sample: "historical beta or systematic risk with respect to the market; historical non-market risk or specific industry and company effects; and the perceived familiarity with the company and its stock" (McDonald and Stehle, 1975, p. 14).

Influential risk perception studies in behavioral accounting

Several studies identify accounting ratios and other information to determine common stocks' perceived risk. Farrelly and Reichenstein (1984) examine six financial risk characteristics from Value Line, a financial publishing company providing investment research and data on various securities. Responses from 209 financial analysts about their risk perceptions on 25 stocks reveal the best proxies of risk perception are safety, a subjective risk factor, and price stability, an objective risk factor. The top objective measures are beta and price stability, explaining 68 percent of the variation in perceived risk. The leading measures of subjective risk are safety and dispersion of analysts' forecasts, explaining 91 percent of the variation in perceived risk.

Farrelly et al. (1985) use seven accounting factors from Beaver et al. (1970) as a basis for evaluating the risk perception of experts: (1) dividend payout, (2) asset growth, (3) leverage, (4) liquidity, (5) asset size, (6) variability of earnings, and (7) co-variability of earnings. These accounting-oriented risk variables explain 79 percent of the risk perception variation among the experts surveyed. The three most significant risk measures are leverage, variability of earnings, and the current ratio (i.e., liquidity). The findings support the notion that financial reports provide useful measures of the perceived riskiness of stocks.

Farrelly et al. (1987) examine 15 financial ratios that might explain risk perceptions for common stocks. Their model includes these seven most significant variables:

one liquidity measure (current ratio),

one turnover ratio (receivables turnover),

two return ratios (profit margin and return on equity), and

three other ratios (the debt ratio, times interest earned, and book value per share).

Their findings reveal that these accounting-related risk factors resulted in an 82 percent success rate in predicting respondent risk perceptions.

International perspectives

Some research examines the role of risk perception within international stock markets. Mear and Firth (1988) use 38 portfolio managers to rate the risk of 30 New Zealand stocks using accounting ratios. The authors report that six accounting-determined risk measures account for 75 percent for the subject's risk perception: (1) net assets, (2) the proprietorship ratio, (3) the liquid ratio, (4) sales growth, (5) dividend coverage, and (6) profitability. They conclude that accounting reports contain some relevant data to assess *ex ante* risk.

Ferris et al. (1990) use data from Farrelly et al. (1985) and include additional data to compare investors in the United States and Japan regarding their risk perceptions. The Japanese survey assesses the perceived risk for 25 stocks by 203 security analysts. The significant explanatory factors are asset growth, leverage, and variability of earnings. The findings show that the accounting data explain the average risk perceptions of security analysts in the United States and Japan. However, the variables have much lower explanatory power for Japanese financial analysts for several reasons. The authors conclude that Japanese investors place less emphasis and dependence on firm performance because they view accounting risk measures as less important. Also, Japanese investors exhibit a higher frequency of insider trading. Lastly, more speculative trading occurs in Japan.

Incorporating Beaver et al.'s (1970) seven accounting-related variables, Capstaff's (1991) study reveals that these factors explain 61 percent of the risk perception of 322 U.K. investment analysts. The two most significant descriptive factors are earnings variability and the current ratio.

Accounting data in the United States, the United Kingdom, and Japan convey risk information differently. Accounting variables explain 66 percent in the United States, 61 percent in the United Kingdom, and 44 percent in Japan of the variation in the risk perception of financial analysts. Adding beta to the seven accounting factors for the U.K. study increases the explanatory power to 83 percent. The four most significant accounting risk characteristics are beta, earnings variability, the current ratio, and asset size.

Biases and issues influencing perceived risk and risk tolerance

The academic literature discusses various biases and other issues influencing a person's degree of perceived risk and risk tolerance. This section provides a sample of these biases, issues, and major findings.

Familiarity bias

Familiarity bias is when investors have an overpowering emotional attachment to well-known financial assets. Investors perceive these investments as having an inverse relationship between risk and return since they believe familiar securities have lower risk and higher return and unfamiliar securities have higher risk and lower return. Wang et al. (2011) examine the risk perception of 1,200 people from a German-language region of Switzerland regarding investment products. Their main finding is participants perceive less complicated investments as possessing lower perceived risk based on familiarity bias. Also, respondents show a positive emotional reaction to familiar financial assets. For financial professionals, Wang et al. (2011, p. 18) comment: "The clients might overestimate the risk of a certain investment due to their lack of knowledge or underestimate the risk due to their overconfidence of the self-perceived knowledge. To fill the knowledge gap is important for effective risk communication." Chapter 3 provides other applications of familiarity bias.

Affective reactions

Positive and negative emotions significantly affect risk-taking behavior and how people assess risk for financial products and services. For example, Kramer and Weber (2012) show people exhibiting seasonal depression evade financial risk-taking during seasons with a decline in daylight hours. However, individuals are more willing to accept riskier investment choices in the spring and summer months, when there are more daylight hours. Grable and Roszkowski (2008) assess how mood affects financial risk tolerance. Their study investigates two premises within the risk tolerance literature. The *mood maintenance hypothesis* (MMH) asserts that a negative (positive) mood increases (decreases) a person's risk tolerance. The *affect infusion model* (AIM) states that a negative (positive) mood decreases (increases) one's risk tolerance. The authors report that respondents made assessments according to the AIM hypothesis.

Rubaltelli et al. (2010) examine how a person's emotional response to different types of mutual funds affects the decision to sell them. The researchers asked respondents to evaluate a socially responsible and a standard mutual fund and specify the price at which they would be willing to sell each fund. The findings reveal that selling prices influence people's feelings about specific mutual funds. Where people had negative affective reactions toward mutual funds, whether socially responsible or standard, this resulted in the highest selling prices. This finding reveals that only people with negative expectations about a financial asset are prone to contradict aspects of the *disposition effect* (i.e., the tendency to sell winning investments too early and hold on to losing investments too long). Investors with positive reactions to a non-socially responsible mutual fund anchor on their initial impressions. However, they do not sell losing funds as quickly as those experiencing negative emotions.

Worry

MacGregor et al. (1999) evaluate investor judgments toward various financial products and asset classes, especially an expert's risk and return perceptions. The data collected are based on questionnaire responses from 265 financial professionals giving their assessment of 19 asset classes based on 14 variables. Some variables are psychological factors, such as knowledge and worry (i.e., how an individual reacts toward a financial situation that causes anxiety or fear). Others involve judgment factors, such as risk perception, return perception, and the likelihood of investing in the financial asset. The authors find that three significant factors – knowledge, worry, and volatility – explain 98 percent of respondents' risk perception.

Trust

Olsen (2012) evaluates the association between perceived risk, trust, and cumulative market risk premiums based on more than 600 responses from a survey of American Association of Individual Investors (AAII) members. He finds an inverse relation between trust and risk perception toward financial securities. Olsen (2012, p. 311) also finds that "ex-ante estimated common stock risk premiums and ex-post market interest rates vary inversely with national trust levels." Additionally, risk premia and interest rates are lower in countries with higher levels of interpersonal trust.

Loss aversion and risk tolerance

Loss aversion is a major aspect of how investors perceive risk. Heilar et al. (2001) study U.K. managers' attitudes to risk and uncertainty in relation to risk management practices. The authors examine companies' risks, investigate the different judgments taken in specific instances, and identify manager risk perceptions and viewpoints. Their findings show that U.K. business managers tend to concentrate on loss aversion rather than risk aversion. Of the 14 major risk characteristics identified by these managers, the two that concerned them the most involve a behavioral perspective of risk: (1) the potential of incurring a future loss and (2) loss-averse behavior. The most prevalent conventional measure of risk is the standard deviation of outcomes.

Family birth order

Another topic within the risk tolerance literature is how sibling order influences an individual's risk tolerance. For example, Gilliam and Chatterjee (2011) report that firstborns have considerably less financial risk tolerance than later-born siblings. Additionally, later-born men are more likely than firstborns to hold mainly stock portfolios. Later-born men are also more prone than later-born women to own a larger percentage of their investments in stocks. Brown and Grable (2015) report that only children and firstborns have lower risk tolerance levels. In other words, these two cohorts are likely less risk tolerant than later-born family members.

Generational risk-taking behavior

Another theme in the academic literature concerns the risk-taking behavior of members within a generational cohort. Rabbani et al. (2021) investigate the connection between *sensation seeking* (i.e., a personality trait that enjoys excitement and adventure) and control in assessing the risk tolerance of "pre-retiree baby boomers." Their findings show that the cohort not identified as sensation seekers prefers an external locus of control (i.e., they believe an outcome occurs because of luck or destiny) and has a low risk tolerance. By contrast, sensation seekers prefer an internal locus of control (i.e., they believe an outcome occurs because they are responsible for their success) and have a high risk tolerance.

Evidence shows that economic shocks and financial crises depress risk-taking behavior among different age cohorts and generations (Malmendier and Nagel, 2011). Gilliam et al. (2010) report that older-aged boomers (i.e., those born between 1946 and 1950) have less financial risk tolerance than younger-aged boomers (i.e., those with birth dates between 1960 and 1964). When examining the risk-taking behavior of Generation X (i.e., those born between 1964 and 1980), Schooley and Worden (2003, p. 58) find that its members have "a low propensity for risk-taking, have an attitude of risk avoidance, and a low capacity for risk." These differences are essential for financial professionals to understand, so that they can figure out how best to communicate with different generational cohorts about risk.

Perceived versus actual risk

Another important research topic is how people assess and process the differences between potential and actual risks. Dessaint and Matray (2017) examine how executives respond to hurricane shocks when their companies located close to this catastrophic event. The authors report that this unexpected event increases managers' perceived risk. In response, they increase their company's cash and disclose hurricane risk in their company financial reports. Real risk is unaffected, and managers' perceived risk eventually declines. Dessaint and Matray (2017, p. 97) conclude, "The distortion between perceived and actual risk is large, and the increase in cash is suboptimal."

Hoffmann et al. (2015) examine how changes in an individual's return perceptions, perceived risk, and risk tolerance influence real trading decisions and risk judgments. Individuals with increasing return expectations trade more frequently, have higher turnover rates, trade larger amounts for each transaction, and use derivatives. People with increasing risk tolerance trade more often, have higher buy–sell ratios, execute limit orders more regularly, and own portfolios with riskier investments. Individuals with higher levels of risk perception trade more often, have greater turnover, have lower buy–sell ratios, and own riskier portfolios.

Hoffmann and Post (2017) investigate how retail investors from the Netherlands revise their assessments about perceived risk and expected returns along with their risk tolerance level as an outcome of their investment history. The authors report that the previous returns of investors have a positive association with their risk tolerance and return expectations and a negative relation with risk perception. Hoffmann and Post (2017, pp. 759–760) conclude, "even in a highly volatile stock market period in which risk appears very salient, investors do not take it into account when updating their beliefs and preferences."

Four aspects of the marketing mix

Singh and Bhowal (2011) apply a well-established marketing concept to how people judge a stock investment's riskiness. They assess the risk perception of employees in relation to common stock by considering aspects of the traditional marketing mix (i.e., product, promotion, price, and place). The authors evaluate how these marketing components can affect how individuals perceive risk for equity shares. The findings show that price is the most significant marketing mix component for measuring a person's risk perception, followed by product, promotion, and place.

Summary and conclusions

Risk assessment is a multi-dimensional process based on financial service or investment product characteristics. Risk encompasses objective and subjective factors that influence investors. Perceived risk and risk tolerance affect how individuals evaluate the information for various financial choices and influence their final investment decision. The academic literature on risk perception documents three critical bases on which individuals' risk perceptions depend: accounting data, traditional risk measures, and behavioral factors. The risk tolerance literature reveals two main themes, namely socioeconomic factors and behavioral issues. Evidence from emerging areas of research also shows that, among others, birth order and generation effects influence risk-taking behavior. Financial professionals and their clients should be aware of these issues to improve risk assessment, investment advice, and client outcomes.

References

Ashton, Robert, and Alison Ashton (ed.). 1999. *Judgment and Decision-Making Research in Accounting and Auditing*. New York: Cambridge University Press.
Beaver, William H., Paul Kettler, and Myron Scholes. 1970. "The Association between Market Determined and Accounting Determined Risk Measures." *Accounting Review* 45:4, 654–682.

Birnberg, Jacob, and Jeffrey Shields. 1989. "Three Decades of Behavioral Accounting Research: A Search for Order." *Behavioral Research in Accounting* 1:1, 23–74.

Brown, Jennifer M., and John E. Grable. 2015. "Sibling Position and Risk Attitudes: Is Being an Only Child Associated with a Person's Risk Tolerance?" *Journal of Financial Therapy* 5:2, 19–36.

Capstaff, John. 1991. "Accounting Information and Investment Risk Perception in the UK." *Journal of International Financial Management and Accounting* 3:2, 189–200.

Dessaint, Olivier, and Adrien Matray. 2017. "Do Managers Overreact to Salient Risks? Evidence from Hurricane Strikes." *Journal of Financial Economics* 126:1, 97–121.

Farrelly, Gail E., Kenneth R. Ferris, and William R. Reichenstein. 1985. "Perceived Risk, Market Risk, and Accounting Determined Risk Measures." *Accounting Review* 60:2, 278–288.

Farrelly, Gail E., Phillip Levine, and William R. Reichenstein. 1987. "Perceptions of Risk Classes: A Discriminant Analysis Using Financial Ratios." *Akron Business and Economic Review* 18:2, 78–91.

Farrelly, Gail E., and William R. Reichenstein. 1984. "Risk Perceptions of Institutional Investors." *Journal of Portfolio Management* 10:4, 5–12.

Ferris, Kenneth, Kazuo Hiramatsu, and Keiichi Kimoto. 1990. "Accounting Information and Investment Risk Perception in Japan." *Journal of International Financial Management and Accounting* 1:3, 232–243.

Gilliam, John, and Swarn Chatterjee. 2011. "The Influence of Birth Order on Financial Risk Tolerance." *Journal of Business and Economics Research* 9:4, 43–50.

Gilliam, John, Swarn Chatterjee, and Dandan Zhu. 2010. "Determinants of Risk Tolerance in the Baby Boomer Cohort." *Journal of Business and Economics Research* 8:5, 79–87.

Grable, John E. 2008. "Risk Tolerance." In Jing Jian Xiao (ed.), *Handbook of Consumer Finance Research*, 3–19. New York: Springer.

Grable, John E., and Michael J. Roszkowski. 2008. "The Influence of Mood on the Willingness to Take Financial Risks." *Journal of Risk Research* 11:7, 905–923.

Heilar, Christine, Alasdair Lonie, David Power, and Donald Sinclair. 2001. *Attitudes of UK Managers to Risk and Uncertainty*. Edinburgh: The Institute of Chartered Accountants of Scotland.

Hoffmann, Arvid O. I., and Thomas Post. 2017. "How Return and Risk Experiences Shape Investor Beliefs and Preferences." *Accounting and Finance* 57:September, 759–788.

Hoffmann, Arvid O. I., Thomas Post, and Joost M. E. Pennings. 2015. "How Investor Perceptions Drive Actual Trading and Risk-Taking Behavior." *Journal of Behavioral Finance* 16:1, 94–103.

Hofstedt, Thomas, and James C. Kinard. 1970. "A Strategy for Behavioral Accounting Research." *Accounting Review* 45:1, 38–54.

Kramer, Lisa A., and J. Mark Weber. 2012. "This Is Your Portfolio on Winter: Seasonal Affective Disorder and Risk Aversion in Financial Decision Making." *Social Psychological and Personality Science* 3:2, 193–199.

Libby, Robert, and Peter C. Fishburn. 1977. "Behavioral Models of Risk Taking in Business Decisions: A Survey and Evaluation." *Journal of Accounting Research* 15:2, 272–292.

Littell, David A., Kenn B. Tacchino, and David M. Cordell. 2003. *Financial Decision Making at Retirement*. Bryn Mawr, PA: The American College.

MacGregor, Donald G., Paul Slovic, Michael Berry, and Harold R. Evensky. 1999. "Perception of Financial Risk: A Survey Study of Advisors and Planners." *Journal of Financial Planning* 12:8, 68–86.

Malmendier, Ulrike, and Stefan Nagel. 2011. "Depression Babies: Do Macroeconomic Experiences Affect Risk Taking?" *Quarterly Journal of Economics* 126:1, 373–416.

Martinussen, Monica, and David R. Hunter. 2009. *Aviation Psychology and Human Factors*. Boca Raton, FL: CRC Press.

McDonald, Jack G., and Richard Stehle. 1975. "How Do Institutional Investors Perceive Risk?" *Journal of Portfolio Management* 2:1, 11–16.

Mear, Ross., and Michael Firth. 1988. "Risk Perceptions of Financial Analysts and the Use of Market and Accounting Data." *Accounting and Business Research* 18:72, 335–339.

Olsen, Robert. 2012. "Trust: The Underappreciated Investment Risk Attribute." *Journal of Behavioral Finance* 13:4, 308–313.

Rabbani, Abed G., Zheying Yao, Christina Wang, and John E. Grable. 2021. "Financial Risk Tolerance, Sensation Seeking, and Locus of Control among Pre-retiree Baby Boomers." *Journal of Financial Counseling and Planning* 32:1, 146–157.

Ricciardi, Victor. 2004. "A Risk Perception Primer: A Narrative Research Review of the Risk Perception Literature in Behavioral Accounting and Behavioral Finance." Working Paper. Available at https://ssrn.com/abstract=566802.

Ricciardi, Victor. 2008a. "Risk: Traditional Finance versus Behavioral Finance." In Frank J. Fabozzi (ed.), *The Handbook of Finance, Volume 3: Valuation, Financial Modeling, and Quantitative Tools*, 11–38. Hoboken, NJ: John Wiley & Sons, Inc.

Ricciardi, Victor. 2008b. "The Psychology of Risk: The Behavioral Finance Perspective." In Frank J. Fabozzi (ed.), *The Handbook of Finance, Volume 2: Investment Management and Financial Management*, 85–111. Hoboken, NJ: John Wiley & Sons, Inc.

Roszkowski, Michael J., and Geoff Davey. 2010. "Risk Perception and Risk Tolerance Changes Attributable to the 2008 Economic Crisis: A Subtle but Critical Difference." *Journal of Financial Service Professionals* 64:4, 42–53.

Rubaltelli, Enrico, Giacomo Pasini, Rino Rumiati, Robert Olsen, and Paul Slovic. 2010. "The Influence of Affective Reactions on Investment Decisions." *Journal of Behavioral Finance* 11:3, 168–176.

Schooley, Diane K., and Debra Drecnik Worden. 2003. "Generation X: Understanding Their Risk Tolerance and Investment Behavior." *Journal of Financial Planning* 16:9, 58–63.

Schulaka, Carly. 2012. "Geoff Davey on Risk Tolerance, Risk Perception, and New Standards for the Future." *Journal of Financial Planning* 25:2, 16–19.

Securities and Exchange Commission. 2004. "Determine Your Risk Tolerance." Available at http://www.sec.gov/investor/pubs/roadmap/risk.htm.

Securities and Exchange Commission. 2010. "Beginners' Guide to Asset Allocation, Diversification, and Rebalancing." SEC Pub. No. 062 (2/10). Available at https://www.sec.gov/reportspubs/investor-publications/investorpubsassetall ocationhtm.html.

Shefrin, Hersh. 2001. "Do Investors Expect Higher Returns from Safer Stocks than from Riskier Stocks?" *Journal of Psychology and Financial Markets* 2:4, 176–181.

Singh, Ranjit, and Amalesh Bhowal. 2011. "Development of Marketing-Driven Measure of Risk Perception." *Journal of Risk Finance* 12:2, 140–152.

Trimpop, Rüdiger M. 1994.*The Psychology of Risk Taking Behavior*. Amsterdam: North-Holland.

Wang, Mei, Carmen Keller, and Michael Siegrist. 2011. "The Less You Know, the More You Are Afraid of a Survey on Risk Perceptions of Investment Products." *Journal of Behavioral Finance* 12:1, 9–19.

3   Heuristics and behavioral biases

... people rely on a limited number of heuristic principles which reduce the complex tasks of assessing probabilities and predicting values to simpler judgmental operations. In general, these heuristics are quite useful, but sometimes they lead to severe and systematic errors.
–Amos Tversky and Daniel Kahneman (1974, p. 1124)

Introduction

The basis of standard finance is classical decision theory, where people are unbiased and maximize their self-interests. This approach assumes that individuals are rational. Being rational requires applying unlimited processing power to all available information and making optimal choices with internally consistent preferences to maximize an action's benefit. Classical decision theory explains how people should make decisions involving uncertainty. However, decades of research show that classical decision theory does not explain how people make decisions. Individuals suffer from many constraints on their cognitive capacity and time, making the necessary decision functions difficult and impractical. Thus, they make decisions without all available information and the necessary cognitive power.

To make judgments under these constraints, people employ heuristics. *Heuristics* are mental shortcuts that can facilitate problem-solving and probability judgments. These mental strategies are rules-of-thumb that reduce the cognitive load otherwise needed. Heuristics are important and effective for making direct judgments. Nevertheless, they often result in irrational and predictably biased conclusions. This chapter begins by reviewing Tversky and Kahneman's (1974) original heuristics, then describes other behavioral biases, and ends with cultural biases.

Heuristics

Heuristic simplification is a process the brain uses to reduce the complexity of analyzing information and making decisions. Tversky and Kahneman (1974) identify three types of heuristics: (1) availability, (2) representativeness, and (3) anchoring and adjustment.

Availability heuristic

Tversky and Kahneman (1973) propose that people use the *availability heuristic* to estimate an event's frequency or probability by the ease with which they can remember past occurrences. They use this mental shortcut to assess an event's probability quickly. However, the memories that come to mind more easily may not represent the bigger picture and thus lead to biases. Thakor (2015) uses the availability heuristic to explain financial crises. Bankers often attribute good banking outcomes to their skills. After a long sequence of good outcomes, these successes become the ones most easily remembered. Bankers, regulators, and investors underestimate the probability of a negative outcome and rush in to purchase high-risk loans and other products. A financial crisis ensues when adverse outcomes finally occur.

Representativeness heuristic

A person's brain processes information with heuristic simplification and concludes that things sharing similar qualities are alike. People mistake a clean car for one that runs well. They attribute the positive qualities of a clean car to its engine, about which they may have little knowledge. Thus, the *representativeness heuristic* involves estimating an event's likelihood by comparing it to an existing prototype already existing in one's mind. Investors may attribute the positive qualities of a good company to it being a good investment. However, investors may overprice a firm's characteristics that generate solid earnings and high sales growth. Thus, it might not be a good investment prospect (Lakonishok et al., 1994). Extrapolation bias is a subset of the representativeness heuristic.

- *Extrapolation bias.* People often extrapolate a past trend into the future because they believe that the past represents the future. Investors tend to buy after a recent increase in the stock market, not after a decline. Bange (2000) shows that when asked about their prediction of the stock market's direction, investor responses correlate more with what happened recently than with what actually occurred.

Anchoring and adjustment heuristic

The *anchoring and adjustment heuristic* is a process of making judgments under uncertainty by first anchoring on information that readily comes to mind due to its availability and then adjusting it until reaching a plausible estimate. Since the process involves choosing an anchor and adjusting, two potential sources of bias are possible.

People anchor on the first value that comes to mind. However, the availability heuristic influences this initial value, which may not produce an answer based on all available knowledge and could be irrelevant to the task at hand. For example, Tversky and Kahneman (1974) review experiments in which participants begin by spinning a wheel of numbers from zero to 100. The researchers then ask them questions about percentages, like estimating the percentage of African countries that are members of the United Nations. A strong link occurs between the estimates and the initial spin result of the wheel. Thus, individuals anchor their initial guess to the spin value and then try to adjust despite no association between the spin result and the question topic.

Finance and economics involve many forecasts and predictions. For example, experts forecast macroeconomic variables, interest rates, stock market expected returns, and company earnings. Campbell and Sharpe (2009, p. 370) "find broad-based and significant evidence that professional consensus forecasts are indeed anchored toward the recent past values of the series being forecasted." In addition, forecast errors are partly predictable, consistent with anchoring on the past.

In the adjustment phase, people often get stuck on the initial anchor. Large deviations between the anchor and the correct answer result in an insufficient adjustment. Thus, the adjusted value is biased in favor of the initial anchor value. Epley and Gilovich (2006) demonstrate that adjustments tend to be deficient because they require significant mental effort. To minimize that effort, a person stops adjusting the value once the estimation falls within a range of plausible values. Therefore, estimates are biased to lie near the anchor side of the implicit range. People can reduce the magnitude of the adjustment-based anchoring bias if given the incentive to exert more effort.

Prospect theory

Traditional expected utility theory (EUT) dominated economic thinking as the accepted normative model. It states that when deciding under uncertainty, people choose the option that gives them the highest weighted average utility over all outcomes. Kahneman and Tversky (1973) illustrate that EUT is limited as a descriptive model and offer *prospect theory* as a better explanation of behavior. They developed prospect theory based on the cognitive heuristics in the previous section.

Investors first frame the decision via choices of potential gains and losses relative to a specific reference point. They often anchor the reference point on the purchase price, given its availability. However, investors could adjust it to other easily remembered values like a recent high or low. They can value the resulting gain or loss through the S-shaped prospect utility function. The S-shape comes from the prospect theory utility function being concave in the gains region, meaning that investors are pleased to earn $5,000 but happier to earn $10,000, though not twice as happy. Therefore, investors prefer earning $5,000 each on two stocks rather than $10,000 on one stock. The prospect utility curve is convex in the loss region, meaning people do not feel twice the pain when suffering twice the loss. The utility curve is also steeper for losses than for gains. Thus, the pain of a loss is greater than the pleasure of a similar magnitude gain. Because of these differences in utility between gains and losses, investors either segregate or combine trades to maximize their happiness over time. For example, Lim (2006) shows that if an investor plans to sell both a winner and a loser, the investor will sell the two assets together if the gain in the winner stock exceeds the loss in the loser stock. Otherwise, the investor will sell the two assets separately on different days.

Disposition effect

The *disposition effect* is the tendency for investors to sell winners too soon and hold losers too long in the portfolio (Shefrin and Statman, 1985). The implication is that this behavior is detrimental to investors. Odean

(1998) illustrates that the stocks sold for higher than their purchase price (winners) continued to beat the market index for months. Thus, investors sold their stock too early. However, the stocks in the portfolio with prices lower than their purchase price (losers) continued to underperform the market index for months. Thus, they should have sold the loser stocks instead of the winner stocks. In the United States, realizing capital gains triggers a tax liability, so selling winners is costlier than selling losers. Although researchers have extensively studied the disposition effect for individual stock investors, they also find this bias in mutual fund trades (Cici, 2012), futures traders (Choe and Eom, 2009), employee stock options (Heath et al., 1999), and real estate (Genesove and Meyer, 2001).

Shefrin and Statman (1985) framed the disposition effect as an outcome of prospect theory. However, others question whether prospect theory is the underlying driver (Kaustia, 2010) and instead offer regret aversion. With *regret aversion*, people feel the emotional pain of regret when they realize that a previous decision was wrong. They take preemptive actions and decisions to avoid feeling this pain. For example, people tend to pick the same lottery numbers because they would regret choosing different numbers and seeing the original numbers win. Odean (1998) shows that investors avoid selling their losing stocks because they would feel the regret of making the wrong choice to purchase the stocks (i.e., the disposition effect). Investors repurchase a stock in which they made an earlier profit but do not repurchase them until they have realized a loss (Strahilevitz et al., 2011). They do not want to relive that regret.

Behavioral biases

People often rely on basic judgments and preferences to simplify complex decisions. The heuristics documented by Tversky and Kahneman (1974) capture some deviations from acting rationally. This section highlights other cognitive approaches that may lead to suboptimal outcomes.

Self-image

People typically view themselves favorably. For example, they consider themselves intelligent, knowledgeable, and friendly. Evidence contradicting this image causes cognitive distress. The following biases allow people to feel better about themselves.

- *Cognitive dissonance.* People are uncomfortable with conflicting beliefs and thus cognitively act to avoid such conflicts. Psychologists refer to this feeling as *cognitive dissonance.* People use confirmation bias to avoid cognitive dissonance. *Confirmation bias* is the tendency to process information by looking for or interpreting information consistent with personal beliefs. Thus, they manipulate their beliefs by rejecting, debunking, or avoiding new information that conflicts with them and by selecting sources of information likely to confirm them. Akerlof and Dickens (1982) suggest specific strategies to avoid cognitive dissonance: (1) ignore, reject, or minimize a memory or belief, (2) change one or both of the ideas so that they match better, or (3) add a third, related idea that can attenuate the dissonance.
  - A primary consequence of cognitive dissonance is inhibiting people from learning from their past. For example, Goetzmann and Peles (1997) show that memory of a past investment performance adapts to enhance self-image. They illustrate that investors report that their past portfolio performance beat the market index when in reality it underperformed it.
  - In a similar study, Glaser and Weber (2007) show that German investors overestimated their past returns. The difference between their estimated return and actual return exceeded 10 percentage points. When investors believe they performed better than they really did, they have no incentive to seek out their mistakes and learn to do better. One way investors can resolve their cognitive dissonance is to blame others for their poor performance. Chang et al. (2016) show that investors have difficulty admitting that past stock purchases were mistakes. However, they are willing to admit and rectify past mutual fund mistakes because they can blame the manager for the poor performance.
- *Confirmation bias.* As previously noted, this bias is the tendency for people to focus on evidence that fits with existing beliefs. For example, Park et al. (2013) study how people use information from message boards to make stock return forecasts. If investors are biased and not objective in valuing information, they will value messages conforming to their prior beliefs. However, they will devalue or ignore messages inconsistent with their previous beliefs. The authors find that investors exhibit substantial confirmation bias despite opportunities to update

prior beliefs, leading to forecasting errors. Those with the strongest prior beliefs display the highest confirmation bias, resulting in greater discrepancies between stock forecasts and actual stock returns.

- *Endowment effect.* People tend to value items they own more highly than they would if they did not own them (Thaler, 1980). In economic experiments, sellers charge more for an item than they would pay if they did not own it. The reason is that people become attached to objects and are affected by the pain associated with giving them up. Consequently, people hold on to their collectible baseball cards, collector pins, and favorite stocks because they develop an emotional attachment.

Familiarity

People often believe that something familiar is better than something unfamiliar. This description refers to *familiarity bias*. Since many stocks and mutual funds are available, people need cognitive processes to narrow the opportunities. Thus, they focus on familiar investments. When reviewing stocks in an industry, investors tend to pick the most familiar stock because they believe it is better. For example, despite the availability of many public utility stocks, people tend to own the one that services their home area (Nofsinger and Varma, 2012).

Although the familiar seems better, the idea of better in finance usually means a higher expected return and lower risk. However, standard finance theory asserts that expected return positively relates to risk. Thus, investors typically do not find low-risk opportunities offering high expected returns. Employees are most familiar with the company that employs them. Benartzi (2001) discusses surveys that ask people which they believe is a riskier investment, owning the company's stock for which they work, or holding a diversified index, such as holding the stocks in the S&P 500 Index. Less than 20 percent identify owning a single company as riskier than holding a diversified index. Familiarity influenced most people to believe their company was better and, thus, less risky. The ramifications are significant. Benartzi reports that companies invest a third of retirement contribution plan funds in company stock. Many employees have lost their jobs and retirement savings after their firms went bankrupt because they invested entirely in company stock that became worthless.

Familiarity bias has the following biases associated with it.

- *Home bias*. Individual and professional investors overweight domestic stocks relative to their proportion of the world equity market (French and Poterba, 1991; Coval and Moskowitz, 2001). Americans allocate more to U.S. equity in their portfolios than justified by the country's share of world equity. Japanese and German investors overinvest in their respective countries. Capital controls, exchange rate risks, and different tax treatments of domestic and foreign stocks cannot explain home bias. Instead, informational advantages and familiarity contribute to the preferences. Thus, many consider home bias an outcome of familiarity bias. Investors favor domestic stocks because they are more familiar with them. When foreigners move to a new country, they initially exhibit significantly lower home bias, but their portfolio allocations converge to the home bias of the new country's citizens over time (Florentsen et al., 2020).

- *Local bias*. Like those who overinvest in domestic firms, investors also overinvest in local firms. Ivković and Weisbenner (2005) report that U.S. individual investors invest on average 30 percent of their portfolio in companies headquartered within 250 miles of their current location. When they move to another geographic location, these investors reduce ownership in the companies near their prior residence and increase ownership in companies close to their new home (Bodnaruk, 2009). Professional investor portfolios also exhibit local bias (Coval and Moskowitz, 1999).

- *Name fluency*. People are more comfortable investing in companies with familiar names. Green and Jame (2013) measure the English fluency of U.S. company names. They find that the more fluent the name, the greater the ownership breadth, trading volume, and valuation. Changing a company name to a more fluent one benefits ownership, volume, and valuation. Similarly, investors prefer mutual funds whose manager names are not foreign.

Overconfidence

Overconfidence is a cognitive bias that describes the tendency to be too confident in the accuracy of one's judgments, resulting in underestimating risks and exaggerating abilities. Much early finance literature on overconfidence studied investors. Investing entails gathering information, analyzing it, and deciding a course of action. Overconfident investors misinterpret the information's accuracy and overestimate their ability to analyze it. Barber and Odean (2001a) show that overconfident investors want to use their knowledge and skills and thus trade too much. Excessive trading degrades their returns (Barber and Odean, 2000). Traditional finance urges investors to maximize returns while minimizing the risk taken. Since overconfident investors underestimate risks, they often take too much risk by owning riskier assets and under-diversifying their portfolios.

Overconfidence also affects corporate finance. Chief executive officers (CEOs) and chief financial officers (CFOs) make many corporate decisions. To reach those positions, they must have developed higher levels of confidence based on past success. These conditions can lead to overconfidence. Companies with overconfident managers take more risks, like using more debt. Their actions are also more optimistic as they make more capital investments, including overpaying for acquisitions. Chapter 9 discusses corporate behavioral finance in more detail.

Three biases are associated with overconfidence.

- *The illusion of control.* People believe they have greater control over events than they do (Presson and Benassi, 1996). For instance, most people choose lottery numbers instead of relying on random selection. People are more likely to bet on the flip of a coin if someone asks them to place the bet before flipping the coin. Active involvement is an important attribute, and past success exacerbates the illusion. During a bull market, investors attribute trading success to their abilities. Thus, they become overconfident, trade more often, allocate more funds toward riskier assets, and use *margin*, the money borrowed from a broker to purchase an investment (Barber and Odean, 2001b).
- *The illusion of knowledge.* This bias is the tendency for people to believe that their decisions improve with more information (Peterson and Pitz, 1988). It mistakes information for knowledge or even wisdom. For example, learning the past few rolls of a dice provides information but does not improve knowledge about outcomes for the next roll. Modern technology and the Internet provide investors with access to considerable data. But having such access does not lead to wisdom without the skills to interpret the data. Access to these data provides an illusion of knowledge leading to overconfidence (Tumarkin and Whitelaw, 2001).

- *Self-attribution bias.* Self-attribution bias leads people to believe that their successes are attributed to their actions and skill, while bad luck causes failure. Self-attribution bias and successes can lead to overconfidence. Consider financial analysts, whose job is to publicize their predictions about future firm earnings. Hilary and Menzly (2006) examine the predictions of analysts over time. Do analyst predictions change relative to other analysts after a series of accurate earnings estimates? After analyzing over 40,000 quarterly earnings forecasts, the authors report that past success leads to predictions deviating from other analysts' estimates and having more significant errors. The analysts became overconfident.

Limited cognitive resources

People have limited cognitive resources to deploy at any given time, called *bounded rationality*. Sometimes individuals may not have enough cognitive ability to complete a mental task. In other cases, they have the ability but must allocate cognitive attention toward the task while limiting attention to other tasks. People must often make decisions even when limited by time, cognitive ability, distractions, poor concentration, and flawed memory. Many behavioral biases stem from processes needed to overcome these cognitive deficits.

- *Alphabeticity bias.* When reviewing investment choices, people tend to allocate more money to choices listed earlier in the menu, which are often ordered alphabetically. Jacobs and Hillert (2016) show that employees are more likely to select the funds appearing toward the beginning of the retirement plan list. These funds may be neither the best ones in their categories nor optimal for the employee.
- *Base rate fallacy.* This bias places too little weight on the original or base rate of possibility and too much on information on a specific company or person. For example, an analyst is assessing the energy industry. One company has historically consistent growth rates and an outstanding management team. Recently, the firm announced a weak quarter. The analyst ignores the firm's base rate successes and decides based on the recent and potentially transient performance.
- *Gambler's fallacy.* This cognitive error is the belief that past occurrences influence the probability of a random future event. For example, the past results from flipping a coin or rolling dice do not affect the next flip or roll. Yet people believe in *mean reversion*, which describes

the phenomenon where if someone gets an extreme value relative to the average, the second number from the same distribution is likely to be closer to the average. For example, if three heads have occurred in coin flips, people often believe that the next flip is more likely to be tails. This fallacy is related to the *law of small numbers*, which is the incorrect belief that small samples ought to resemble the population from which someone draws them (Rabin, 2002).

- *Longshot bias.* People overvalue the riskiest bets in most betting markets because they overweight low-probability events (Snowberg and Wolfers, 2010). In gambling environments like horse racing and sports betting, gamblers value longshots too much, given how rarely they win, and value favorites too little. They are systematically poor at distinguishing between small and tiny probabilities, like 0.01 percent and 0.0001 percent, consequently valuing them nearly equally. As a result, they bet and lose too much money on longshots.

- *Naïve allocation* or *naïve diversification.* When allocating investments in a defined contribution plan, people often use the 1/n heuristic and equally divide the contribution among the available options (Benartzi and Thaler, 2001). When the options available skew toward one asset class, like equities, naïve portfolios may also be skewed (Huberman and Jiang, 2006). For example, when five options are available, a participant allocates 20 percent of the contribution to each one. If three of the five options are for stock mutual funds, participants allocate 60 percent to equities without making a conscious decision. When many investment options are available, people tend to eliminate some and divide the contribution equally to the remaining choices (Baltussen and Post, 2011).

- *Salience bias* or *attention bias.* Investors focus on news and information that grabs their attention and is noteworthy. Conversely, they ignore information that does not catch their attention. This bias has a profound impact on investors. Given many stocks, which ones should an investor buy? Barber and Odean (2008) illustrate that individual investors buy stocks with *attention-grabbing news*, defined as stocks with unusually high volume, extreme returns, or news coverage. Barber and Odean (2008, p. 813) report "… that individual investors display attention-driven buying behavior. They are net buyers on high-volume days, following both extremely negative and extremely positive one-day returns, and when stocks are in the news."

- *Status quo.* This bias describes a preference for accepting the current situation. It is associated with procrastinating about making decisions and resisting change (Samuelson and Zeckhauser, 1988). This procrastination causes employees to postpone making retirement plan contribution decisions so long that they may never participate in the plan (Madrian and Shea, 2001).

Other behavioral biases

Many other biases do not fit neatly into the previous categories. Psychologists and behavioral economists continue to discover new biases and cognitive errors.

- *Mental accounting.* As discussed in Chapter 1, people tend to compartmentalize money into different mental accounts (Thaler, 1984). For example, they may have vacation, retirement, and housing money. Also, how people earn money places it in a mental account that helps determine how they spend it. For instance, individuals spend gambling winnings differently than their paychecks. They treat year-end bonuses differently than regular paychecks. Investors also treat each investment asset as a separate mental account. This narrow framing of their investments is a key aspect of prospect theory and the disposition effect mentioned earlier.

However, mental accounting complicates fully diversifying portfolios. Investors think about each asset's return characteristics in isolation and not the interaction (correlation) between asset returns. *Correlation* is a statistical measure expressing the linear relation between two variables. It is the key characteristic of diversification, but the concept does not come to mind easily because it requires analysis across separate mental accounts (Agnew et al., 2003).

Another diversification problem is that people match their investment assets to the goals of each mental account (Shefrin and Statman, 2000). For example, people might invest their retirement money primarily in equities. Money saved for a down payment on a house might be in all cash assets. This process of investing for individual goals may not result in an optimal portfolio. Other difficulties created by mental accounting are executing tax swaps and tax-loss selling. A *tax swap* is selling an asset at a loss to reduce the tax liability and buying a similar asset so that the portfolio continues to have the same characteristics. *Tax-loss selling* is selling assets at a loss near the end of the calendar year to reduce tax liability.

- *Sunk cost fallacy.* Traditional finance dictates that people consider present and future costs and benefits when deciding on a course of action. However, they also consider past costs. A *sunk cost* is a cost that has already occurred and has no potential for recovery in the future. Thus, sunk costs should be irrelevant in financial decision-making. Business examples include marketing, research and development, and training expenses. People tend to escalate an endeavor once they invest their money or time (Arkes and Blumer, 1985). After making one or more investments in a project that turns out badly, people become motivated to make further investments to save it.
- *Visual biases.* Some behavioral biases are triggered visually. Financial analysis is often displayed visually, yet the display can create biases. For example, the *left-digit bias* occurs because people judge the difference between $5.00 and $3.99 to be larger than that between $5.01 and $4.00, even though the differences are the same (Sokolova et al., 2020). Another example is using the color red. Bazley et al. (2021) illustrate how using red to represent financial data affects individuals' perceptions. Specifically, their risk preferences, expectations of future stock returns, and trading decisions are affected.

Cultural biases

Culture plays a vital role in finance by influencing choice over the long term. What is culture? Stulz and Williamson (2003, p. 314) define culture as the "transmission from one generation to the next, via teaching and imitation, of knowledge, values, and other factors that influence behavior." Common ways to measure culture are through language, ethnicity, religion, and values. These measures lead to a level of trust. For example, Guiso et al. (2003, 2008) show that religion and ethnicity influence trust. In turn, trust influences savings behavior and economic outcomes. Higher levels of trust lead to more economic trade and higher savings behavior.

The Hofstede measures of cultural values are the most used in the literature (Hofstede, 1980). Obtained from surveys, the five dimensions of culture are (1) power distance between people with and without power, (2) individualistic versus collectivistic society, (3) uncertainty avoidance, measuring how well people deal with anxiety, (4) masculinity versus femininity, referring to the distribution of roles between men and women, and (5) long- versus short-term orientation, dealing with the time horizon people in a society display. Chui et al. (2010) use these measures to assess culture's impact on trading. They report that countries with higher levels of individualism display higher trading volume and higher return volatility. Culture is also related to higher momentum profits. The authors contend that individualism is related to overconfidence and self-attribution bias.

Summary and conclusions

When making an economic decision under uncertainty, people do not behave as if they are using classical decision theory. Comparatively, their decisions may seem irrational. Behavioral finance recognizes that people suffer from many constraints on their cognitive capacity and time, making the necessary decision functions difficult and impractical. Thus, they use cognitive heuristics and behavioral biases to cope. Although these heuristics and biases allow people to function and make decisions, they can also lead to suboptimal decisions. People's cultural origins can sometimes influence their decision-making.

References

Agnew, Julie, Pierluigi Balduzzi, and Annika Sundén. 2003. "Portfolio Choice and Trading in a Large 401(k) Plan." *American Economic Review* 93:1, 193–215.

Akerlof, George A., and William T. Dickens. 1982. "The Economic Consequences of Cognitive Dissonance." *American Economic Review* 72:3, 307–319.

Arkes, Hal, and Catherine Blumer. 1985. "The Psychology of Sunk Cost." *Organizational Behavior and Human Decision Processes* 35:1, 124–140.

Baltussen, Guido, and Gerrit T. Post. 2011. "Irrational Diversification: An Examination of Individual Portfolio Choice." *Journal of Financial and Quantitative Analysis* 46:5, 1463–1491.

Bange, Mary. 2000. "Do the Portfolios of Small Investors Reflect Positive Feedback Trading?" *Journal of Financial and Quantitative Analysis* 35:2, 239–255.

Barber, Brad, and Terrance Odean. 2000. "Trading Is Hazardous to Your Wealth: The Common Stock Investment Performance of Individual Investors." *Journal of Finance* 55:2, 773–806.

Barber, Brad, and Terrance Odean. 2001a. "Boys Will Be Boys: Gender, Overconfidence, and Common Stock Investment." *Quarterly Journal of Economics* 116:1, 261–292.

Barber, Brad, and Terrance Odean. 2001b. "The Internet and the Investor." *Journal of Economic Perspectives* 15:1, 41–54.

Barber, Brad, and Terrance Odean. 2008. "All that Glitters: The Effect of Attention and News on the Buying Behavior of Individual and Institutional Investors." *Review of Financial Studies* 21:2, 785–818.

Bazley, William J., Henrik Cronqvist, and Milica Mormann. 2021. "Visual Finance: The Pervasive Effects of Red on Investor Behavior." *Management Science* 67:9, 5616–5641.

Benartzi, Shlomo. 2001. "Excessive Extrapolation and the Allocation of 401(k) Accounts to Company Stock." *Journal of Finance* 56:5, 1747–1764.

Benartzi, Shlomo, and Richard H. Thaler. 2001. "Naive Diversification Strategies in Defined Contribution Saving Plans." *American Economic Review* 91:1, 79–98.

Bodnaruk, Andriy. 2009. "Proximity Always Matters: Local Bias when the Set of Local Companies Changes." *Review of Finance* 13:4, 629–656.

Campbell, Sean D., and Steven A. Sharpe. 2009. "Anchoring Bias in Consensus Forecasts and Its Effect on Market Prices." *Journal of Financial and Quantitative Analysis* 44:2, 369–390.

Chang, Tom Y., David H. Solomon, and Mark M. Westerfield. 2016. "Looking for Someone to Blame: Delegation, Cognitive Dissonance, and the Disposition Effect." *Journal of Finance* 71:1, 267–302.

Choe, Hyuk, and Yunsung Eom. 2009. "The Disposition Effect and Investment Performance in the Future Market." *Journal of Futures Markets* 29:6, 496–522.

Chui, Andy C. W., Sheridan Titman, and K. C. John Wei. 2010. "Individualism and Momentum around the World." *Journal of Finance* 65:1, 361–392.

Cici, Gjergji. 2012. "The Prevalence of the Disposition Effect in Mutual Funds' Trades." *Journal of Financial Quantitative Analysis* 47:4, 795–820.

Coval, Joshua D., and Tobias J. Moskowitz. 1999. "Home Bias at Home: Local Equity Preference in Domestic Portfolios." *Journal of Finance* 54:6, 2045–2073.

Coval, Joshua D., and Tobias J. Moskowitz. 2001. "The Geography of Investment: Informed Trading and Asset Prices." *Journal of Political Economy* 109:4, 811–841.

Epley, Nicholas, and Thomas Gilovich. 2006. "The Anchoring and Adjustment Heuristic: Why the Adjustments Are Insufficient." *Psychological Science* 17:4, 311–318.

Florentsen, Bjarne, Ulf Nielsson, Peter Raahauge, and Jesper Rangvid. 2020. "Turning Local: Home-Bias Dynamics of Relocating Foreigners." *Journal of Empirical Finance* 58:September, 436–452.

French, Kenneth R., and James M. Poterba. 1991. "Investor Diversification and International Equity Markets." *American Economic Review* 81:2, 222–226.

Genesove, David, and Christopher Meyer. 2001. "Loss Aversion and Seller Behavior: Evidence from the Housing Market." *Quarterly Journal of Economics* 116:4, 1233–1260.

Glaser, Markus, and Martin Weber. 2007. "Why Inexperienced Investors Do Not Learn: They Do Not Know Their Past Portfolio Performance." *Finance Research Letters* 4:4, 203–216.

Goetzmann, William, and Nadav Peles. 1997. "Cognitive Dissonance and Mutual Fund Investors." *Journal of Financial Research* 20:2, 145–158.

Green, T. Clifton, and Russell Jame. 2013. "Company Name Fluency, Investor Recognition, and Firm Value." *Journal of Financial Economics* 109:3, 813–834.

Guiso, Luigi, Paola Sapienza, and Luigi Zingales. 2003. "People's Opium? Religion and Economic Attitudes." *Journal of Monetary Economics* 50:1, 225–282.

Guiso, Luigi, Paola Sapienza, and Luigi Zingales. 2008. "Trusting the Stock Market." *Journal of Finance* 63:6, 2557–2600.

Heath, Chip, Steven Huddart, and Mark Lang. 1999. "Psychological Factors and Stock Option Exercise." *Quarterly Journal of Economics* 114:2, 601–627.

Hilary, Gilles, and Lior Menzly. 2006. "Does Past Success Lead Analysts to Become Overconfident?" *Management Science* 52:4, 489–500.

Hofstede, Geert. 1980. *Culture's Consequence*. New York: Sage Publications.

Huberman, Gur, and Wei Jiang. 2006. "Offering versus Choice in 401(k) Plans: Equity Exposure and Number of Funds." *Journal of Finance* 61:2, 763–801.

Ivković, Zoran, and Scott Weisbenner. 2005. "Local Does as Local Is: Information Content of the Geography of Individual Investors' Common Stock Investment." *Journal of Finance* 60:1, 267–306.

Jacobs, Heiko, and Alexander Hillert. 2016. "Alphabetic Bias, Investor Recognition, and Trading Behavior." *Review of Finance* 20:2, 693–723.

Kahneman, Daniel, and Amos Tversky. 1973. "Prospect Theory: An Analysis of Decision under Risk." *Econometrica* 47:2, 263–292.

Kaustia, Markku. 2010. "Prospect Theory and the Disposition Effect." *Journal of Financial and Quantitative Analysis* 45:3, 791–812.

Lakonishok, Josef, Andrei Shleifer, and Robert Vishny. 1994. "Contrarian Investment, Extrapolation, and Risk." *Journal of Finance* 49:5, 1541–1578.

Lim, Sonya Seongyeon. 2006. "Do Investors Integrate Losses and Segregate Gains? Mental Accounting and Investor Trading Decisions." *Journal of Business* 79:5, 2539–2573.

Madrian, Brigitte, and Dennis Shea. 2001. "The Power of Suggestion: Inertia in 401(k) Participation and Savings Behavior." *Quarterly Journal of Economics* 116:4, 1149–1187.

Nofsinger, John R., and Abhishek Varma. 2012. "Individuals and Their Local Utility Stocks: Preference for the Familiar." *Financial Review* 47:3, 423–443.

Odean, Terrance. 1998. "Are Investors Reluctant to Realize Their Losses?" *Journal of Finance* 53:5, 1775–1798.

Park, JaeHong, Prabhudev Konana, Bin Gu, Alok Kumar, and Rajagopal Raghunathan. 2013. "Information Valuation and Confirmation Bias in Virtual Communities: Evidence from Stock Message Boards." *Information Systems Research* 24:4, 1050–1067.

Peterson, Dane, and Gordon Pitz. 1988. "Confidence, Uncertainty, and the Use of Information." *Journal of Experimental Psychology* 14:1, 85–92.

Presson, Paul, and Victor Benassi. 1996. "Illusion of Control: A Meta-Analytic Review." *Journal of Social Behavior and Personality* 11:3, 493–510.

Rabin, Matthew. 2002. "Inference by Believers in the Law of Small Numbers." *Quarterly Journal of Economics* 117:3, 775–816.

Samuelson, William, and Richard Zeckhauser. 1988. "Status Quo Bias in Decision Making." *Journal of Risk and Uncertainty* 1:1, 7–59.

Shefrin, Hersh, and Meir Statman. 1985. "The Disposition to Sell Winners Too Early and Ride Losers Too Long: Theory and Evidence." *Journal of Finance* 40:3, 777–790.

Shefrin, Hersh, and Meir Statman. 2000. "Behavioral Portfolio Theory." *Journal of Financial and Quantitative Analysis* 35:2, 127–151.

Snowberg, Erik, and Justin Wolfers. 2010. "Explaining the Favorite–Long Shot Bias: Is It Risk-Love or Misperceptions?" *Journal of Political Economy* 118:4, 723–746.

Sokolova, Tatiana, Satheesh Seenivasan, and Manoj Thomas. 2020. "The Left-Digit Bias: When and Why Are Consumers Penny Wise and Pound Foolish?" *Journal of Marketing Research* 57:4, 771–788.

Strahilevitz, Michal Ann, Terrance Odean, and Brad M. Barber. 2011. "Once Burned, Twice Shy: How Naïve Learning, Counterfactuals, and Regret Affect the Repurchase of Stocks Previously Sold." *Journal of Marketing Research* 48:SPL, S102–S120.

Stulz, René M., and Rohan Williamson. 2003. "Culture, Openness, and Finance." *Journal of Financial Economics* 70:3, 313–349.

Thakor, Anjan. 2015. "Lending Booms, Smart Bankers, and Financial Crises." *American Economic Review: Papers and Proceedings* 105:5, 305–309.

Thaler, Richard. 1980. "Toward a Positive Theory of Consumer Choice." *Journal of Economic Behavior and Organization* 1:1, 39–60.

Thaler, Richard. 1984. "Mental Accounting and Consumer Choice." *Marketing Science* 4:3, 199–214.

Tumarkin, Robert, and Robert F. Whitelaw. 2001. "News or Noise? Internet Postings and Stock Prices." *Financial Analysts Journal* 57:May/June, 41–51.

Tversky, Amos, and Daniel Kahneman. 1973. "Availability: A Heuristic for Judging Frequency and Probability." *Cognitive Psychology* 5:2, 207-232.

Tversky, Amos, and Daniel Kahneman. 1974. "Judgment under Uncertainty: Heuristics and Biases." *Science* 185:4157, 1124–1131.

4   Cognition and intelligence

You don't need to be a rocket scientist. Investing is not a game where the guy with the 160 IQ beats the guy with 130 IQ.
—Warren Buffett (Carol Loomis, 2012, p. 101)

Introduction

What is intelligence? People think of intelligence as the capacity to learn and apply knowledge and skills. This chapter describes the different types of intelligence and relates them to investing and financial decisions. Do people exhibit fewer behavioral biases when they are smart?

Scholars have identified three kinds of cognitive ability: fluid intelligence, theory of mind, and cognitive reflection. High ability in one does not necessarily mean high ability in the others. The definitions of the three forms of intelligence are as follows.

- *Fluid intelligence* is a person's reasoning ability. A standard measure of fluid intelligence is the intelligence quotient (IQ), a gauge scaled to a society average of 100. Finance has a high degree of complexity. Thus, people with higher IQs may be suitable to handle those complex decisions.
- *Theory of mind* is a person's ability to infer the intentions of others. Finance involves many people, like analysts, bankers, chief financial officers (CFOs), and portfolio managers. Being able to infer their intentions can be helpful.
- *Cognitive reflection* is the tendency to use a slower, more analytical cognitive process instead of a quicker, intuitive one. Intuition often uses heuristics to facilitate more rapid decisions. A more analytical process is more likely to avoid behavioral biases.

Cognitive processing and finance

The opening chapter quote by Warren Buffet suggests that intelligence matters for finance, but it may only matter to a certain degree. However, Mr. Buffet only mentions fluid intelligence. He is missing the theory of mind and cognitive reflection.

IQ and finance

People have been taking IQ tests for decades, often to apply for a university or when entering military service. Thus, scholars can compare a person's investment choices to their IQ test results. The following studies suggest that people with higher fluid intelligence are more likely to invest in the stock market, take more risks, and be more successful investors.

Grinblatt et al. (2011) use the IQ tests completed by all Finnish men for their mandatory military service. Finland had a wealth tax that required the listing of all assets. By merging the IQ data with tax returns data, these researchers assessed the relationship between fluid intelligence and stock market participation. They sorted men into nine IQ categories (lowest to highest) and examined each group's percentage of people invested in the stock market. The results show a positive relationship between intelligence and stock market participation. Only 9.8 percent of the lowest IQ group invested in the stock market. Participation rates increased monotonically to 46.5 percent in the highest IQ group. Statistical analysis shows that IQ explains the stock market participation rate more strongly than income, wealth, or other characteristics. Additionally, high-IQ men chose more diversified portfolios.

Grinblatt et al. (2012) merged the Finnish men's IQ data with stock trading and portfolio data to assess whether IQ was important in investment returns. They report that higher IQ investors:

- outperformed the low IQ investors' portfolios by 4.9 percentage points a year,
- were better at buying low and selling high (market timing),
- bought better-performing stocks (i.e., they had stock-picking skills),
- sold stocks with losses at the end of the year to lower their taxes (tax-loss selling), and

- were less prone to the *disposition effect*, the tendency to hold losers too long and sell winners too soon.

Grinblatt et al. (2016) conducted a similar analysis with the Finnish IQ data and mutual fund choices, focusing on the fees associated with funds. Mutual fund costs have an inverse correlation with fund return performance. They report that high IQ investors paid lower mutual fund fees by avoiding actively managed and high-cost fund categories. These investors purchased shares directly with the fund rather than through expensive retail networks.

D'Acunto et al. (2021) examined the Finnish data in combination with the Consumer Survey of Statistics Finland to assess cognitive ability's role in inflation forecasting. The survey asked a constant sample of approximately 1,500 Finns monthly about general economic conditions and inflation expectations. To compute the forecast error, the authors compared the predicted 12-month inflation rate to the realized inflation rate. The study found that high-IQ men (i.e., those with IQ above the median) displayed 50 percent lower forecast errors and were less likely to round their estimates and forecast implausible values.

Lastly, Dohmen et al. (2010) conducted an experiment using 952 German adults to examine their levels of financial risk aversion and time impatience and relate them to cognitive ability. A series of choices between a paid lottery and a safe payment estimated the participants' willingness to take risks. Similarly, a series of questions that included a choice between accepting 100 euros now versus X euros in 12 months measured the time impatience. The series of time questions varied the value of X. The amount (X) for which the participant would choose to wait 12 months for the larger payment indicated the level of impatience. They concluded that people with higher intelligence were significantly less risk-averse and less impatient than people with low intelligence. Lower risk aversion and lower time impatience are consistent with traits needed for investing in the stock market.

In summary, compared to people with low fluid intelligence, people with higher IQ:

- were more likely to invest in the stock market,
- were better investors (i.e., better able to time the market and pick better-performing stocks, and create better portfolios),

- were more likely to use tax-loss selling techniques,
- provided better inflation predictions,
- demonstrated lower risk aversion and lower time impatience, and
- exhibited fewer behavioral biases.

The theory of mind and finance

Reading an opponent is essential for negotiations. Whether negotiating a venture capital deal, a merger, or a compensation contract, inferring the information and needs of an opponent improves the outcome. Assessing an opponent uses the theory of mind cognitive process, which is the capacity to imagine other people's intentions.

The best way to examine the theory of mind is to have people interact in an experiment. Bruguier et al. (2010) designed an experiment where participants traded with one another as a group. Participants could hold cash and buy and sell two risky assets. Each asset could pay dividends of between $0 and $0.50, with the combined value being $0.50. The dividend values are unknown, but the fact that those dividends have a negative correlation is known. If one dividend is higher, the other must be lower. The research design gave some participants inside information about one of the dividend values. For example, the researchers informed one participant that asset B's dividend would be above $0.35, making it more valuable because asset A would have a dividend of $0.15 or less. The uninformed participants knew there were informed traders among them. However, participants with high theory of mind cognitive processing may be able to infer who the informed traders were by watching their trades and placing similar trades. After running the experiment with different participants, the scholars report that people are good at inferring information from the order flow. Despite their lack of formal financial training, the uninformed participants correctly forecasted the price direction of the two risky assets two-thirds of the time. This finding indicates that they correctly identified the informed trader and inferred which was the more valuable asset.

Two traditional tests for theory of mind intelligence commonly used in experiments do not rely on human interaction. In the first experiment, a researcher shows a movie clip with geometric shapes moving to imitate social interaction. After stopping the movie clip, the researcher asks the participants to predict the shapes' subsequent movements. In the second experiment, the Reading the Mind in the Eyes Test (RMET), a researcher asks participants to view pictures of people's eye gazes and infer their mood by selecting from four mental states. Ridinger and McBride (2015) show that women generally score higher on the RMET than men. However, when money incentivizes the RMET, men score equally as well as women.

Bruguier et al. (2010) used an IQ test (to measure fluid intelligence) and the two theory of mind tests in a price forecasting experiment. Price forecasting success was more related to theory of mind cognitive processing than the math test used as a subcategory of an IQ test. The researchers also conducted brain imaging of participants using functional magnetic resonance imaging (fMRI). Their results show that theory of mind originates in the frontal and medial parts of the cortex, the most developed part of the brain.

Cognitive reflection and finance

Kahneman (2011) describes two different modes of cognitive reasoning. *Thinking fast* refers to the intuitive thinking mode that relies on feelings, heuristics, and past experiences to make decisions. *Thinking slow* refers to reasoning, also known as the *analytical cognitive process*. While the intuitive mode of thinking is spontaneous and effortless (fast), analytical thought is deliberate and takes effort (slow). Everyone can think either way. People tend to default to one mode more than the other. *Cognitive reflection* is the ability to take the time needed before deciding.

Measuring Cognitive Reflection

Researchers often measure cognitive reflection using Frederick's (2005) three-question test, referred to as the *cognitive reflection test* (CRT). The questions immediately tempt an impulsive wrong answer, consistent with intuitive thinking. A person needs analytical cognitive processing to overcome that impulse and get the correct answer. The CRT provides scores between 0 (strongly intuitive) and 3 (strongly analytical) correct answers. The questions are:

1. If it takes 5 machines 5 minutes to make 5 widgets, how long would it take 100 machines to make 100 widgets?

2. In a lake, there is a patch of lily pads. Every day, the patch doubles in size. If it takes 48 days for the patch to cover the entire lake, how long would it take for the patch to cover half the lake?
3. A bat and ball together cost $1.10. The bat costs $1.00 more than the ball. How much does the ball cost?

In the first question, the symmetry of the 5, 5, and 5 followed by the 100, 100 leads to the impulsive answer of 100. However, the correct answer is 5 minutes. In the second question, the terms "doubles" and "half" lead the reader to half the 48 days to answer 24 days. However, the correct answer is 47 days, so it can double and cover the entire lake on the 48th day. In the third question, the costs of $1.10 and $1.00 elicit the impulsive answer of $0.10. However, the ball must cost $0.05 and the bat $1.05 to have a $1.00 difference. As the original three-question CRT became too well known, Toplak et al. (2014) designed four additional questions that researchers can use independently or with the original three.

Cognitive Reflection and Behavioral Biases

Intuitive thinking is more susceptible to psychological biases because it uses more heuristics than the analytical thinking mode. Hoppe and Kusterer's (2011) survey of 414 university students demonstrates this situation. They measured the students' cognitive reflection and susceptibility to the base rate fallacy. The *base rate fallacy* occurs when placing too little weight on the initial rate of possibility and too much weight on recent occurrences.

Consider this question: "In a city with 100 criminals and 100,000 innocent citizens, a surveillance camera exists with automatic face recognition software. If the camera sees a known criminal, it triggers the alarm with a 99 percent probability; if the camera sees an innocent citizen, it triggers the alarm with a probability of 1 percent. What is the probability of filming a criminal when the alarm is triggered?"

The quick and intuitive answer of 90 percent or more is common but incorrect. This result comes from the 99 percent hit rate probability for criminals. However, the criminal population is small. A false positive, or a false alarm, for the sizeable innocent population is more important than the intuitive thinker realizes. Consider what would happen if everyone in town walked by the camera. It would trigger an alarm 99 times (= 99 percent × 100) for the criminals and 1,000 times (= 1 percent × 100,000) for the non-criminals. Thus, the camera would be correct 99 times out of 1,099 or about 9 percent. The students who responded that the probability was 10 percent or less had higher CRT scores.

Instead of students, Nofsinger and Varma (2011) surveyed over 100 financial planners to determine how cognitive reflection relates to risk aversion and prospect theory. According to *prospect theory*, people tend to choose the sure option when framed positively (making money) and the risky option when framed negatively (losing money). The authors split the planner group into two groups by CRT score for analysis. The intuitive planner exhibited risk aversion in the positive and risk-seeking in the negative frames. This result is consistent with prospect theory. However, the analytical planners tended toward the opposite behavior. Most exhibited risk-seeking in the positive domain and risk aversion in the negative domain.

These two papers conclude that people who tend toward a cognitive reflective process exhibit less behavioral bias.

The three cognitive processes and finance

Research shows that fluid intelligence, theory of mind, and cognitive reflection influence financial decisions. Do these cognitive processes work together, or are they independent? Do they affect financial decisions similarly, or do they influence different aspects? Corgnet et al. (2018) conducted an experiment to assess these questions. They engaged 167 people to participate in 17 rounds of computerized trading. Participants traded an asset that could have one of three values. No one knew what the value would be, but everyone had private information about one value the asset could not take. Through observing the trading, a person might learn the information others had.

Besides the trading exercise, the researchers measured each participant's IQ, theory of mind, and cognitive reflection. The study reached the following conclusions by relating these cognitive measures to trades and profits.

- Fluid intelligence was important for modeling asset value.
- Theory of mind was associated with inferring the information content of trades.

- A connection occurs between cognitive reflection, exhibiting fewer behavioral biases, and adjusting trades to the inferred information of others.

All three cognitive abilities are critical in finance, but for different reasons. The quantitative skills associated with fluid intelligence are essential for valuation. Theory of mind abilities help to interpret market signals. Cognitive reflection helps to avoid behavioral biases and mental errors.

Cognitive aging

Cognitive aging is the gradual decline of reasoning, memory, and processing speed. It peaks at around age 20 and then declines by 1 percent annually through age 80 (Agarwal et al., 2009). Making sound financial decisions takes both cognitive ability and experience. Although youth brings high cognitive function, age brings experience. Cognitive aging and gaining experience are two opposing influences. The peak of financial decision ability tends to be around age 50. After 70, the propensity for financial mistakes accelerates.

Korniotis and Kumar (2011) illustrate the dual impacts of cognitive decline and investment experience by examining the portfolio holdings and trades of over 62,000 investor accounts. They use age as a proxy for cognitive ability and the length of time the brokerage account was open as a proxy for experience. The study compares age and experience to investment performance, diversification, and trading. It reports:

- Older investors hold less risky portfolios.
- Experience is associated with better diversification, less trading, more tax-loss selling, and fewer behavioral biases.
- Cognitive aging is associated with worse stock selection ability and poor diversification.
- Investment skill deteriorates sharply, starting at 70, resulting in an estimated 3 percentage points lower risk-adjusted annual return.

Two ramifications of cognitive aging are the decline in financial literacy and the susceptibility to being victimized by fraud. Finke et al. (2017) used the Consumer Finance Monthly survey to measure the financial literacy of 3,873 people over 60. The survey implemented the Financial Literacy

Assessment Test, which asked four questions in each of the categories of basic finance, credit, insurance, and investing. The financial literacy score demonstrates the decline in financial literacy: 62 percent for the 60 to 69 age group, 49 percent for the 70 to 79 age group, and 32 percent for 80 and over seniors. An unfortunate outcome of cognitive aging is that people do not lose confidence in their financial ability. Confidence in managing their finances increased from 72 percent in the 60 to 69 age group to 74 percent in the over 80 age group. Thus, people who have lost much cognitive ability and financial literacy may not seek professional advice.

The study also examined overconfidence and the propensity to take risks to break even in the context of financial fraud. *Overconfidence* is a behavioral bias occurring when a person's subjective confidence in their ability exceeds their actual performance. The survey asked participants how they thought they did on the financial literacy test. An answer greater than their actual test score indicated overconfidence. Overconfidence played an essential role in becoming a financial fraud victim. A one-third increase in overconfidence increased the odds of being scammed by 26 percent. After losing, some people are willing to take more risks to break even. The elderly participants increased their risk aversion over the period. However, the fraud victim subsample slightly decreased their risk aversion. This tendency makes them more susceptible to a "follow-up" scam offer to get their money back for a substantial fee.

Older investors who have experienced cognitive decline may need more protection from fraud. However, the U.S. regulatory system may cause many to be more vulnerable because they qualify as an accredited investor due to their wealth level. The U.S. government allows accredited investors to trade securities that are unregistered with financial authorities, like hedge funds and private equity. Finke et al. (2021) find that accredited households of age 80 and older are far less likely to score as well on financial literacy tests as people in their early 60s. Thus, they are unlikely to be sophisticated investors as intended by the accredited investor definition.

Summary and conclusions

Intelligence is critical for making sound financial decisions. The three forms of cognitive ability are fluid intelligence, theory of mind, and cognitive reflection. High ability in one does not necessarily mean high ability in the others. The quantitative skills associated with fluid intelligence are essential for valuation. Theory of mind abilities help interpret market signals, and cognitive reflection helps avoid behavioral biases and mental errors. Cognitive ability declines with age. This tendency causes older people to lose some financial literacy and be more susceptible to behavioral biases and fraud.

References

Agarwal, Sumit, John C. Driscoll, Xavier Gabaix, and David Laibson. 2009. "The Age of Reason: Financial Decisions over the Life Cycle with Implications for Regulation." *Brookings Papers on Economic Activity* 2:Fall, 51-117.

Bruguier, Antoine J., Steven R. Quarz, and Peter Bossaerts. 2010. "Exploring the Nature of 'Trader Intuition.'" *Journal of Finance* 65:5, 1703-1723.

Corgnet, Brice, Mark DeSantis, and David Porter. 2018. "What Makes a Good Trader? On the Role of Intuition and Reflection on Trader Performance." *Journal of Finance* 73:3, 1113-1137.

D'Acunto, Francesco, Daniel Hoang, Maritta Paloviita, and Michael Weber. 2021. "IQ, Expectations, and Choice." *Review of Economic Studies*, Forthcoming.

Dohmen, Thomas, Armin Falk, David Huffman, and Uwe Sunde. 2010. "Are Risk Aversion and Impatience Related to Cognitive Ability?" *American Economic Review* 100:3, 1238-1260.

Finke, Michael S., John S. Howe, and Sandra J. Huston. 2017. "Old Age and the Decline in Financial Literacy." *Management Science* 63:1, 213-230.

Finke, Michael S., Tao Guo, and Sandra J. Huston. 2021. "The Unsophisticated 'Sophisticated': Old Age and the Accredited Investors Definition." *Financial Planning Review* 4:2, e1114.

Frederick, Shane. 2005. "Cognitive Reflection and Decision Making." *Journal of Economic Perspectives* 19:4, 25-42.

Grinblatt, Mark, Seppo Ikäheimo, Matti Keloharu, and Samuli Knüpfer. 2016. "IQ and Mutual Fund Choice." *Management Science* 62:4, 924-944.

Grinblatt, Mark, Matti Keloharju, and Juhani T. Linnainmaa. 2011. "IQ and Stock Market Participation." *Journal of Finance* 66:6, 2121-2164.

Grinblatt, Mark, Matti Keloharju, and Juhani T. Linnainmaa. 2012. "IQ, Trading Behavior, and Performance." *Journal of Financial Economics* 104:2, 339-362.

Hoppe, Eva I., and David J. Kusterer. 2011. "Behavioral Biases and Cognitive Reflection." *Economics Letters* 110:2, 97-100.

Kahneman, Daniel. 2011. *Thinking, Fast and Slow*. New York: Farrar, Straus, and Giroux.

Korniotis, George M., and Alok Kumar. 2011. "Do Older Investors Make Better Investment Decisions?" *Review of Economics and Statistics* 93:1, 244-265.

Loomis, Carol. 2012. *Tap Dancing to Work: Warren Buffett on Practically Everything, 1966-2012*. New York: Time Inc.

Nofsinger, John, and Abhishek Varma. 2011. "How Analytical Is Your Financial Advisor?" *Financial Services Review* 16:4, 245–260.

Ridinger, Garret, and Michael McBride. 2015. "Money Affects Theory of Mind Differently by Genders." *PloS ONE* 10:12, 1–15.

Toplak, Maggie E., Richard F. West, and Keith E. Stanovich. 2014. "Assessing Miserly Information Processing: An Expansion of the Cognitive Reflection Test." *Thinking and Reasoning* 20:2, 147–168.

5   The human biology of financial decision-making

> *But economics has no near kinship with any physical science. It is a branch of biology broadly interpreted.*
> –Alfred Marshall (1920), founder of the neoclassical school of economics

Introduction

A critical personal attribute of both traditional and behavioral finance is risk aversion. A person's level of risk aversion can dramatically affect their wealth over their lifetime. For example, a person with high risk aversion might select a mostly bond and cash portfolio for their 401(k) retirement plan or other employer-based contribution plan. This conservative approach is likely to yield a much lower final value at retirement than a mostly stock and bond portfolio selected by someone with a lower level of risk aversion. However, what is the source of a person's risk aversion level?

One answer is experience, including education. Experiencing numerous situations provides a context for making decisions with risk and uncertainty. Another possibility is that a person's physiology affects risk aversion. Indeed, examining risk aversion in the context of biology may help to explain why it seems to change over time and from situation to situation. This question of origin is also relevant for psychological biases and cognitive errors. Why do some people exhibit a particular bias while others do not? Again, biology might help explain the observed differences. As Nofsinger and Shank (2020) note, biology influences behavior in a transient (e.g., sleep deprivation, circulating hormones, and mood), quasi-permanent (e.g., physical health and mental health), and permanent (e.g., DNA) manner. This chapter reviews how biology, including genetics, hormones, and health, affects financial and economic decision-making.

Genetics

What drives a person's decisions, nature or nurture? Do people learn to behave the way they do, or does biology drive their behavior? Researchers examine these questions by studying twins and DNA to learn how genetics affect behavioral finance.

Genome

The Human Genome Project determined and mapped the sequence of nucleotide base pairs that make up human DNA. Large-scale investigations to associate specific genes with behavior are now possible. Using molecular genetic information in economics is referred to as "genoeconomics." However, the scale is immense. The human genome has approximately 3 billion nucleotide pairs arranged into 23 chromosomes. Although all humans share 99.6 percent of their genetic variation, the differences still leave hundreds of thousands of genetic markers to explore. Thus, tests with thousands of people and hundreds of thousands of explanatory genome variables will have little power to detect genuine associations.

Making the genome data more manageable requires grouping gene variants. The genome-wide association studies (GWAS) procedure started with the nucleotide pairs in which people may differ, called single nucleotide polymorphisms (SNPs). Researchers individually evaluated the millions of SNPs, with essential controls, against a specific behavior or outcome, like the level of education attained. Most genes were not associated with education. However, findings show a positive association with some gene variants but a negative association with others. The GWAS method combines the influence of all the genes with significant association to the behavior and assigns a polygenic score for that behavior. A *polygenic* score is an index of a person's number of SNPs associated with a given behavior. It is a weighted index that indicates how significant each SNP is to the behavior. Each person will have a polygenic score that researchers can easily use in statistical analysis. Lee et al. (2018) report a gene variant combination for education attainment (EA). Thus, many studies use this EA score, the polygenic score, for education attainment.

The Health and Retirement Study (HRS) survey genotyped its participants. Sias et al. (2020) use EA scores from the HRS to examine how genetics affect stock market participation. The HRS is a data panel of Americans aged 50 and older. The authors find that people with higher EA scores, which they call genetic endowments, are more likely to invest in equity markets and thus invest more of their wealth in risky assets. Barth et al. (2020) also use the HRS survey. They report that the average EA score in a household strongly and robustly predicts wealth at retirement. The gene–wealth association may partially stem from the findings that the EA score relates to risk preferences and mortality. Like the previous study, they report that the scores strongly predict stock ownership. People with lower EA scores reduce their chances of wealth accumulation because they tend to have less accurate beliefs about macroeconomic probabilities and shorter planning horizons.

Genome studies are complex. New methods will allow more research into how genetic endowments affect financial behavior and outcomes.

Twins

Research studies of twins exploit the fact that identical twins (monozygotic twins) come from one egg and one sperm and thus share 100 percent of their genetic material, while fraternal twins (dizygotic twins) result from two eggs and two sperm and therefore, on average, share 50 percent of the genetic material that varies between people. These studies assume that twins will have the same nurturing experience when raised together and have different experiences in adulthood. Through these differences in genetics, early nurturing, and later experiences, scholars can identify the degree to which these three categories explain various financial decisions and outcomes.

The Swedish Twin Registry has identified twins born in Sweden since 1886, registering tens of thousands of identical and fraternal twins. As adults, many of these twins have taken surveys via telephone, mail, and the Internet. Researchers can merge these data with national databases such as those maintained by the Swedish Tax Agency, Premium Pension

Agency, and the military. Using these databases, scholars have investigated the proportion of influence genetics has on financial outcomes.

Barnea et al. (2010) studied the financial portfolio of over 37,000 twins and an equal sample of non-twins using data from the Tax Agency. Before 2006, Sweden had a 1.5 percent annual tax on wealth, and thus citizens reported their assets annually. Consider the investment choice of whether to invest in the stock market. If shared early experiences drive the decision to invest, the decision correlation between identical twins should be the same as that between fraternal twins. However, the correlation between identical twins is more than twice that between fraternal twins, 0.298 versus 0.143, indicating that the decision to invest is more similar between identical twins than between fraternal twins. Since identical twins share the same genetic code, this finding suggests that nature plays a vital role in decision-making.

These researchers assessed the relative degree of influence of each of the three decision sources, namely genetics, nurture (early shared experiences), and unique environment. They report that genetics explain about a third of the decision to invest after controlling for individual characteristics, such as age, income, gender, wealth, and education. The control variables explained less than genetics did. Nurture explained minimal variation in the investment decision, whereas unique experiences explained the other two-thirds.

The study also examined the fraction of the portfolio invested in the stock market. Genetic makeup also explains a portion of this decision. Subsample analysis shows that the portion of the decision explained by genetics to invest a fraction of the portfolio in stocks was:

- 29.0 percent overall,
- 44.5 percent, age < 30,
- 19.2 percent, 30 < age < 55,
- 29.1 and 22.4 percent, men and women, respectively, and
- 38.5 percent, twins reared apart.

Cesarini et al. (2010) studied the twin's investment choices in the national pension system. Before 2000, the Swedish Premium Pension Agency made all investment choices. After 2000, participants could choose among nearly 500 investment funds for their investment account. Most Swedes (68 percent) made an active allocation decision. The findings reveal that genetics explained 28 percent of the level of risk taken. Unique environment experiences defined most of the rest. In addition, they identified the highest return funds (top 10 percent) of their investment category during the previous three years. People often exhibit an *extrapolation bias* (i.e., the belief that the recent trend will persist, which is a form of representativeness bias). The study shows that genetics explains over 30 percent of the extrapolation bias propensity.

Cesarini et al. (2012) also surveyed twins to assess the role of genetics and designed a survey to measure seven psychological biases. The biases, their measurement, and the decisions explained by genetics follow.

- *Sunk cost* (a cost incurred that an individual or firm cannot recover): involves a question about going to a show after losing a ticket, 39 percent.
- *Representativeness bias* (the mistake of believing that two similar things are more closely correlated than they are): involves three questions about the likelihood of people belonging to different groups, 36 percent.
- *Illusion of control* (the tendency for people to overestimate their ability to control events): involves questions about the discount acceptable for choosing one's numbers in a lottery, 24 percent.
- *Status quo bias* (a preference to not undertake any action to change the current state of affairs): involves a question about having switched to cheaper service providers who are newly available, 24 percent.
- *Loss aversion* (the tendency to prefer avoiding losses to acquiring equivalent gains): involves three lottery questions, 23 percent.
- *Procrastination* (delaying or postponing something despite the negative consequences): involves a question about being late paying bills, 18 percent.
- *Time impatience* (willingness to delay receiving a good or benefit): asks about the discount acceptable to receive money sooner, 18 percent.

In summary, a person's genome explains a large portion of the investment decisions and specific biases.

Adoption

Some criticize the twins' studies because they attribute too much variation between identical and fraternal twins to genetics. The heightened communication between identical and fraternal twins could explain some differences. Thus, examining other tests for the role of genetics in investing, such as adoption, is helpful.

Sweden also keeps extensive adoption records. Black et al. (2017) identified adults adopted as children and their adoptive and biological parents. The study compares the adoptee's investment decisions regarding stock market participation and risk aversion with those of the biological and adoptive parents. The similarities to the birth parents' decisions suggest a role for genetics, and the similarities to the adoptive parents' decisions imply that the environment is important. The environment portion resembles the twin studies' combined nurture and unique experiences. The authors conclude that the adoptive parents' effect (environment) has twice the impact on the adoptee's decision to participate in the stock market than the biological parents' effect (genetics). The environmental effect is four times larger than the genetic effect for the level of risk taken, as measured by the portfolio's volatility. Overall, this study of adoptions suggests that genetics does matter, but the environment matters more.

Physiology

Hormones affect mood, emotions, and impulses, thus affecting behavior. Health status and exercise also impact mood and emotions. Thus, it should not be surprising to learn that physiology influences behavioral finance.

Hormones

Hormones have a significant impact on a person's mood and energy level. The major classes of hormones include amines, peptides and proteins, and steroids. Steroids are the focus here. The best-known steroid is testosterone, a male hormone, although women have testosterone in lower measures. Studies reveal that high testosterone levels are associated with riskier behavior in many social contexts. The research explores the possibility that testosterone levels can affect financial decision-making, looking both at current circulating testosterone levels and at levels in utero when forming the brain.

For tests associated with levels in utero, higher exposure to prenatal testosterone leaves measurable impacts on the body. These impacts are visible in adults. For example, body markers are (1) the ratio between the length of the second and fourth fingers (2D:4D) is smaller for people exposed to higher prenatal testosterone, and (2) more testosterone leads to higher masculinity of facial features. Jia et al. (2014) investigated the facial masculinity of chief executive officers (CEOs) and corporate decisions in finance and accounting. They found that facial masculinity is positively associated with risky behavior, such as financial misreporting, option backdating, and insider trading.

Two studies examined the link between participants' 2D:4D finger ratio (and thus testosterone) and financial decision-making, one looking at the association between the ratio and risk aversion and the other the association between the ratio and trading profits. Garbarino et al. (2011) surveyed participants on three risky financial decisions using lottery questions. They concluded that subjects with a smaller 2D:4D ratio (i.e., exposed to higher prenatal testosterone levels) are more willing to take financial risks. This situation occurred for men and women. In the second study, Coates et al. (2009) followed high-frequency male traders from a trading floor in London. The findings report that both the 2D:4D ratio and the number of years of training equally predicted the traders' 20-month trading profitability. Thus, experience and hormones had roughly an even contribution to trading success.

Twin testosterone transfer could be another way in which prenatal testosterone could impact brain and body development. The hypothesis is that for opposite-sex fraternal twins, prenatal testosterone for the male fetus increases the prenatal testosterone exposure of the female fetus. Does this extra testosterone affect the female twin's behavior as an adult? Women tend to be more risk-averse than men. Does the female twin of a female–male pair take more financial risk than other women, all else equal? Cronqvist et al. (2016) use the Swedish Twin Registry to compare the behavior of females from opposite-sex twin pairs to same-sex twin pairs. They conclude that a female twin from an opposite-sex pair tends to allocate more financial assets to equity and invest in a higher-risk portfolio as measured by return volatility. The female twin also allocates a higher proportion of the portfolio to individual stocks relative to mutual funds, trades more often (overconfidence), and owns more lottery-type stocks. Indeed, such female twins take more investment risk.

Health

A fundamental financial theory of risk and return is that taking systematic risk leads to earning risk premiums over the long term. These higher returns can increase the value of an investment portfolio more than a low-risk portfolio over a lifetime. Poor diet and little exercise can contribute to poor health, but do obesity, poor health, diet, and exercise affect financial decisions and outcomes? Unhealthy people will accumulate smaller portfolios if they tend to take lower investment risks. Using U.S. and European retirement data, Addoum et al. (2017) show that obesity influences portfolio choice. Overweight people were less likely to participate in the stock market. When they invest in the stock market, they hold less risky assets due to being less optimistic. The primary drivers of these results were education, cognitive ability, and race.

Using the Survey of Health, Aging, and Retirement in Europe, Bressan et al. (2014) examined the impact of health on portfolio choice. When categorizing health into five groups (poor, fair, good, very good, and excellent), only the poor health group behaved differently from the other groups. The unhealthiest people held low-risk portfolios.

Diet and exercise are factors of health status and affect cognitive function. A diet high in saturated fat and refined sugar negatively influences brain function, while vegetable and fruit consumption have a positive effect. Exercise increases mental activity in the regions related to emotion, memory, risk-taking, problem-solving, and decision-making. Exercise and a better diet can improve mood, influencing financial risk-taking enthusiasm.

Mental illness and substance abuse disorder also affect financial decision-making. Common psychiatric conditions include obsessive-compulsive disorder, depression, anxiety, phobias, and alcoholism. Poor mental health could affect investment and portfolio choices because it may:

- alter cognitive abilities,
- affect the ability to regulate mood and emotion,
- alter a person's degree of risk aversion, and
- decrease the ability to evaluate investment opportunities and reduce available funds for investing through lower productivity and increased medical spending.

Using data from seven biennial waves of the Health and Retirement Survey (HRS), Bogan and Fertig (2013) examined mental health status and household portfolio allocation. Households suffering from mental illnesses decreased their investments in risky investments. Bogan and Fertig (2018) continued their previous work by focusing on how mental illness affected retirement savings accounts. Psychological distress could influence retirement savings through changes to risk preferences or intertemporal discounting. They report that households affected by mental health problems were more risk-averse and had a bias toward a more short-term investment focus.

Wealth effects on biology

Wealthier people are healthier and live longer. The direction of the causation between wealth and health is unclear. More affluent people can buy better health care and afford better food and nutrition. However, good health may allow one to earn a higher income by working longer in the short and long term. Nevertheless, examining wealth shocks helps determine whether wealth changes can cause health changes. The booms and busts in the stock market generate dramatic, unexpected gains and losses in many people's wealth. Do these wealth shocks affect health? Yes, they can influence physical and mental health.

Schwandt (2018) shows that a 10 percent change in lifetime wealth over two years is associated with a change of 2–3 percent of a standard deviation when measuring physical health, mental health, and survival rates of elderly retirees in the United States. The author characterizes the results as suggesting that among 100 retirees losing 10 percent of their remaining lifetime wealth, 2.5 will develop an additional health condition, and one additional retiree will not survive the next two years. Negative stock market returns can cause psychological distress (e.g., anxiety, anger, and frustration) associated with physical symptoms (e.g., high blood pressure, heart attacks, and strokes) and poor decision-making. Engelberg and Parsons (2016) examined patient records from California hospitals and correlated admissions with stock market returns. They report that the day after a large decline in the stock market, the number of people admitted for psychological conditions like panic disorder and major depression increased. Severe psychological distress can lead to suicide.

Wisniewski et al. (2020) used data from the Organisation for Economic Co-operation and Development (OECD) for 36 countries and stock market indices over more than 40 years. They find that declines in the stock market are associated with increases in the suicide rate. The authors use their model coefficients to estimate the number of lives lost from the 2008 stock market crash. Their calculations show that the 2008 stock market crash resulted in an additional 6,566 suicides across the 36 nations between 2008 and 2009.

Do stock market returns affect death? Giuliettia et al. (2020) used fatal car accident data in the United States between 1990 and 2015 along with daily stock market returns to assess whether the stock market can influence emotional states. They find that a one standard deviation reduction in daily stock market returns is associated with a 0.6 percent increase in fatal car accidents that day.

Barnes (2021) examined the deceased organ donor records from the U.S. Health Resources & Services Administration between 1987 and 2018 and correlated the deaths with stock market returns. One key finding is that decreases in daily stock market returns are associated with increases in organ donor deaths the following day. Another finding is that heart attacks and strokes, which are stress-related deaths, are the most sensitive to stock market return shocks. As Barnes (2021, p. 1) notes, "... there is a natural tension between wealth and health even at the extremes of utility, or in other words, death."

Summary and conclusions

What drives behavior, nature or nurture? Both appear to be relevant. Biology influences risk aversion and behavioral bias in transient, quasi-permanent, and permanent ways. This chapter reviews how biology affects financial decision-making through genetics (e.g., genome, twin, and adoption studies), hormones (e.g., circulating and prenatal testosterone), and health (e.g., physical and mental). The chapter also reviews how the financial markets can affect a person's health. Many other biological topics are available to explore themes not covered in this chapter, such as gender, brain function, sleep deprivation, personality, pollution, and more.

References

Addoum, Jawad M., George Korniotis, and Alok Kumar. 2017. "Stature, Obesity, and Portfolio Choice." *Management Science* 63:10, 3393–3413.

Barnea, Amir, Henrik Cronqvist, and Stephan Siegel. 2010. "Nature or Nurture: What Determines Investor Behavior?" *Journal of Financial Economics* 98:3, 583–604.

Barnes, Spencer. 2021. "Killing in the Stock Market: Evidence from Organ Donations." *Journal of Behavioral and Experimental Finance* 32:December, 100563.

Barth, Daniel, Nicholas W. Papageorge, and Kevin Thom. 2020. "Genetic Endowments and Wealth Inequity." *Journal of Political Economy* 128:4, 1474–1522.

Black, Sandra E., Paul J. Devereux, Petter Lundborg, and Kaveh Majlesi. 2017. "On the Origins of Risk-Taking in Financial Markets." *Journal of Finance* 72:5, 2229–2278.

Bogan, Vicki L., and Angela R. Fertig. 2013. "Portfolio Choice and Mental Health." *Review of Finance* 17:3, 955–992.

Bogan, Vicki L., and Angela R. Fertig. 2018. "Mental Health and Retirement Savings: Confounding Issues with Compounding Interest." *Health Economics* 27:2, 404–425.

Bressan, Silvia, Noemi Pace, and Loriana Pelizzon. 2014. "Health Status and Portfolio Choice: Is Their Relationship Economically Relevant?" *International Review of Financial Analysis* 32:3, 109–122.

Cesarini, David, Magnus Johannesson, Paul Lichtenstein, Örjan Sandewall, and Björn Wallace. 2010. "Genetic Variation in Financial Decision-Making." *Journal of Finance* 65:5, 1725–1754.

Cesarini, David, Magnus Johannesson, Patrik K. E. Magnusson, and Björn Wallace. 2012. "The Behavioral Genetics of Behavioral Anomalies." *Management Science* 58:1, 21–34.

Coates, John M., Mark Gurnell, and Aldo Rustichini. 2009. "Second-to-Fourth Digit Ratio Predicts Success among High-Frequency Financial Traders." *Proceedings of the National Academy of Sciences* 106, 623–628.

Cronqvist, Henrik, Alessandro Previtero, Stephan Seigel, and Roderick E. White. 2016. "The Fetal Origins Hypothesis in Finance: Prenatal Environment, the Gender Gap, and Investor Behavior." *Review of Financial Studies* 29:3, 739–786.

Engelberg, Joseph, and Christopher A. Parsons. 2016. "Worrying about the Stock Market: Evidence from Hospital Admissions." *Journal of Finance* 71:3, 1227–1250.

Garbarino, Ellen, Robert Slonim, and Justin Sydnor. 2011. "Digit Ratios (2D:4D) as Predictors of Risky Decision Making for Both Sexes." *Journal of Risk and Uncertainty* 42:1, 1–26.

Giuliettia, Corrado, Mirco Tonind, and Michael Vlassopoulos. 2020. "When the Market Drives You Crazy: Stock Market Returns and Fatal Car Accidents." *Journal of Health Economics* 70:C, 102245.

Jia, Yuping, Laurence Van Lent, and Yachang Zeng. 2014. "Masculinity, Testosterone, and Financial Misreporting." *Journal of Accounting Research* 52:5, 1195–1246.

Lee, James J., Robbee Wedow, Aysu Okbay et al. 2018. "Gene Discovery and Polygenic Prediction from a 1.1-Million-Person GWAS of Educational Attainment." *Nature Genetics* 50:8, 1112–1121.

Marshall, Alfred. 1920. *Principles of Economics.* London: Macmillan. Reprinted by Prometheus Books, 1997.

Nofsinger, John R., and Corey Shank. 2020. *The Biology of Investing: Nature, Nurture, Physiology, and Cognition.* New York: Routledge.

Schwandt, Hannes. 2018. "Wealth Shocks and Health Outcomes: Evidence from Stock Market Fluctuations." *American Economic Journal: Applied Economics* 1:4, 349–377.

Sias, Richard, Laura Starks, and Harry J. Turtle. 2020. "Molecular Genetics, Risk Aversion, Return Perceptions, and Stock Market Participation." Working Paper 27638, National Bureau of Economic Research.

Wisniewski, Tomasz Piotr, Brendon John Lambe, and Keshab Shrestha. 2020. "Do Stock Market Fluctuations Affect Suicide Rates?" *Journal of Financial Research* 43:4, 737–765.

6 Social finance and sentiment

> *Most importantly, there is a need to move from behavioral finance to social finance (and social economics). Social finance includes the study of how social linkages affect information flows, securities markets ... and of how ideologies that affect financial decisions form and spread.*
> –David Hirshleifer (2015, p. 151)

Introduction

Traditional finance states that investors learn by observing market prices. Social finance recognizes that besides prices and beliefs, behaviors are also transmitted via social interaction and are necessary components of the decision process. In this context, information and behavioral biases develop from transmitting feelings and behaviors through personal observation, conversation, mass media, and social media (Akçay and Hirshleifer, 2021).

As illustrated in this chapter, scholars have studied how coworkers, neighbors, and social interaction affect financial decisions. Many studies also examine how the general mood in society, often called *sentiment*, influences behavior and asset prices. Hirshleifer (2020) synthesized this research to form a social, economic, and financial paradigm in his 2020 presidential address to the American Finance Association. The paradigm recognizes that people communicate with each other via talking, written text, and social media. They also observe the actions of others. This social interaction can rapidly transmit information, opinion, and emotion regardless of whether the material transmitted is correct.

Micro-level social interaction

People learn through interacting with and observing others. Conversation is a crucial way to obtain information and detect emotional reactions. Social interaction helps people form opinions.

Peer effects

Social interaction, sometimes called *peer effects*, is particularly impactful for complex ideas and uncertain decisions, like financial decisions. Conversation permits exchanging such information as beliefs on retirement savings, household borrowing and default, stock market participation, and portfolio choice (Kuchler and Stroebel, 2021).

People communicate with their peers at work and at home. They discuss their beliefs about stocks at work and with neighbors at home. Financial professionals, like stockbrokers and analysts, converse with other brokers and analysts. People also share and seek opinions on social media. Egan et al. (2014) call others' views "second-order beliefs" and note that they can impact a person's behavior. For example, if some investors determine that others are more optimistic, they may buy more stocks than their beliefs justified. However, if they believe others are more pessimistic, they may buy fewer stocks for their portfolios.

A survey of individual investors shows that they talk to 20 people on average about a typical investment, while less than a third do any analysis themselves (Shiller and Pound, 1989). Several studies illustrate the influence of one's peers on financial decisions. Hong et al. (2004) predict that peer influence affects highly social people more than less social people. Highly social people interact with others more frequently and for more extended periods. This interaction allows for more exchange of information and opinion. The authors define a *social household* as members interacting with neighbors or attending church. Using the responses from a survey of 7,500 households in the Health and Retirement Study (HRS) of households, they report that social households are more likely to invest in the stock market. In neighborhoods with high stock market participation, stock market investment is even more likely for socially active households. Thus, social interaction has considerable influence in the right environment – one with investors.

Ivković and Weisbenner (2007) contend that stock investing ideas diffuse over neighborhoods through word of mouth. They report that people's stock holdings in the neighborhood strongly influence a household's portfolio. If a neighbor increases purchases in a particular industry by 10 percentage points, the family increases purchases in the same industry by 2 percentage points. This neighborhood effect is more robust for buying local companies. The findings are surprising given that individual investors hold few stocks in their brokerage accounts, where the median is four stocks. Institutional investors have far more stocks in their portfolios, often numbering in the hundreds. Pool et al. (2015) examine professional money managers in the same neighborhood. The managers who share an ethnic background have more similar holdings and trades. Individuals who share a culture likely increase their social interaction.

People in an ethnic or peer group tend to develop similar preferences and interests. These shared beliefs develop into social norms for the peer group. Social norms about financial beliefs help govern whether the peer group values investing. If not, the peer group will rarely discuss the issue, and little social interaction will occur. Duflo and Saez (2002, 2003) show that participation in a defined contribution plan at work highly depends on coworker involvement.

Contagion through a Ponzi scheme

Person-to-person interaction is typically unobservable. Therefore, studies have assumed that neighborly and coworker word-of-mouth information diffusion occurred. Wincapita's Ponzi scheme dynamics illustrate the details of such diffusion. The scheme was active between 2003 and 2008 in Finland. Like other Ponzi schemes, it promised investors substantial returns. At first, Wincapita claimed that the profits came from sports betting, but it later switched the story to currency trading. "Profits" offered to existing investors were the incoming cash flows from new investors, not from sports betting or currency trading. The scheme grew to over 10,000 investors, approximately 0.2 percent of the total population of Finland. In total, scheme operators transferred €100 million from investors to Wincapita, with an average amount invested of €15,100.

Rantala (2019) studied the responses of Wincapita's numerous victims in the ensuing legal investigation. Officials were unaware of this scheme for many years because Wincapita did not advertise publicly. An existing investor had to sponsor new investors. Sponsors received €200 in their investment account and 20 percent of the new investor's profits. This dynamic made Wincapita a word-of-mouth information diffusion scheme. The investigation identified the social networks through which new investors entered the scheme. The diffusion of information occurs rapidly through social networks even when most people share it with only one or two others. This case study offers several conclusions.

- *Credibility matters.* People increased their investments when the sponsor had comparatively higher age, income, and education.
- *Personal relationships matter.* A relative or close friend sponsor increased credibility.
- *The scheme's collapse was emotionally tragic.* People reported destroyed personal relationships, divorces, suicides, and mental health problems.

Social interaction can substantially affect a person's investment beliefs and actions, even when word-of-mouth information dissemination communicates wrong or inaccurate messages.

Macro-level social mood

The micro-level social interaction within neighborhoods, workplaces, and communities can aggregate into a national social mood. The investment industry refers to this fluctuating social mood as *market sentiment*.

Media

People express and transmit ideas and emotions through narratives. They strive to understand events by forming them into a narrative communicated through social interactions. Shiller (2017, p. 968) uses the term narrative to mean "a simple story or easily expressed explanation of events that many people want to bring up in conversation or on news or social media because it can be used to stimulate the concerns or emotions of others, and/or because it appears to advance self-interest." A narrative can be factual or misleading. It can have a national impact when it "goes viral." National narratives create social norms that influence financial actions. In many cases, financial fiduciaries and experts do not have the right to act based on their judgment. Instead, they must follow the narrative of what a prudent person would do in the same situation, known as the *prudent person rule*. That does not provide guidance other than mimicking others' actions or following a prescribed set of decisions, known as a safe harbor script.

The transmission of narratives, information, and opinions mainly occurs through language. Words are inherently more subjective than numbers and thus might influence investor judgment. Word choice can create vibrant images that are emotionally engaging. Do investors react differently to "profits jumped" versus "profits increased"? Hales et al. (2011) show that people are susceptible to hype. They experimented on how positive vibrant words during a bull market and negative vibrant terms during a bear market affected people's predictions. In a bull market scenario, these researchers divided participants into bullish long stock positions and bearish short stock positions. They expected investors with long positions to predict higher future returns than those with short positions. However, how does each respond to vivid versus bland positive news? Investors with long positions give similar predictions after both vivid and bland expressions. However, investors with short positions give higher return predictions when presented with vivid versus bland words. When the researchers framed the experiment in a bear market, the investors with short positions had predictions consistent with the market trend, and investors with long positions predicted a market reversal. In this case, the investors with long positions were sensitive to word choice. The hype seems to affect investors positioned against the trend.

Knowing that hype gains viewers, the news media embellish the news with hyperbole. García (2013) examines the tone of the words in the *New York Times* financial news columns. In over a century of news, stocks fall the following day when the number of negative words in the articles exceeds the number of positive ones. The fraction of negative words is exceptionally high when the market reaches the bottom.

To what degree does social media influence investment decisions? Siikanen et al. (2018) study the trading in Nokia stock, one of the most liquid stocks on the Finnish stock market. Nokia posts announcements on Facebook and Twitter. The authors conclude that Facebook posts influence the buy/sell decisions of unsophisticated investors like households, nonprofits, and less active investors. Facebook posts do not influence more sophisticated investors like financial institutions and active traders, because they may have access to more information sources.

Sentiment

Financial decision-makers experience a level of optimism or pessimism that can affect an outcome. Emotions are correlated across economic participants through social interaction, creating sentiment (Nofsinger, 2005). Investors quickly propagate sentiment to the stock market. Sentiment can be transitory or long term. Shefrin (2005) illustrates how behavioral biases and preferences affect asset prices. The theoretical basis for sentiment is the difference between his behavioral asset pricing model outcomes and traditional model outcomes.

Scholars have explored different sentiment measures for decades. They derived some of the first measures from within the stock market, like the closed-end fund discount (Lee et al., 1991). The difference between the closed-end fund's net asset value and its price is called the *closed-end fund discount*. Some researchers contend that closed-end fund discounts are high when sentiment is pessimistic and low when sentiment is optimistic. Baker and Wurgler (2006) combine several market-related potential sentiment measures, such as the closed-end fund discount, share turnover, the number and average first-day returns on initial public offerings (IPOs), the equity shares in new issues, and the dividend premium, into one sentiment index. Another method to measure sentiment is to simply ask people how they feel and what they plan to do. The University of Michigan's Index of Consumer Expectations measures consumer confidence. The American Association of Individual Investors (AAII) also conducts an Investor Sentiment Survey of its members. State Street surveys institutional investors in its Investor Confidence Index.

Recently, the research trend has been to find measures or sources of social mood outside the investment industry to gauge how it affects investment decisions and asset markets. Examples of short-term sentiment sources are popular sporting events or television (TV) shows. Soccer is the most popular sport in the world. People are passionate about their national team. Edmans et al. (2007) examine 1,100 soccer match outcomes with the next day's stock returns in 39 countries. They report that the losing team's stock market declines an average of 0.21 percent. The magnitude grew as the importance of the match increased. The negative return was larger for countries with a history of soccer success. A similar analysis for cricket and basketball games yields declines of 0.19 and 0.21 percent after losses, respectively. The stock market shows no reaction to team victories. The most popular sport in the United States is American football. Chang et al. (2012) examine the returns of companies headquartered in the city of the winning and losing teams. Stock from the losing team's city underperforms that from the winning city the day after the game by almost 0.06 percent. This effect doubles when the odds-makers favor the losing team to win.

People can also be enthusiastic about the characters in their favorite TV shows. Lepori (2015) examines popular TV season finales and the ensuing stock market reaction. People are sad that their show ends, and the next day the stock market declines. This situation is noteworthy because networks advertise the end of a TV series in advance, so its end is predictable. The study examines 159 series finales from *The Fugitive* in the 1960s to *The Closer* in 2012. A negative association exists between the number of people watching the final episode and the stock market's decline the following day. However, the magnitude is only an 8 basis point decline for every 20 percent increase in viewership.

Music choice reflects a person's mood. For example, sad people listen to sad music to express their emotions, and happy people listen to happy songs. Edmans et al. (2022) create a music-based sentiment measure in 40 countries using Spotify, the leading online music platform worldwide. Spotify tracks the songs streaming in each country and provides daily statistics of the top 200 songs. An algorithm classifies a song's positivity or valence. An index of the valence of the daily top 200 songs measures the mood of each country's citizens. By comparing the country's valence index with its equity market, the researchers find a positive relation between music sentiment and concurrent market returns. Specifically, Edmonds et al. (2022, p. 2) note, "A one-standard-deviation increase in music sentiment is associated with a higher weekly return of 8.1 basis points, or 4.3 percent annualized." A significant price reversal occurred the following week. In addition, music sentiment predicts increases in net mutual fund flows and decreases in government bond returns. Thus, music sentiment is a proxy for transient sentiment.

Obaid and Pukthuanthong (2022) examine the photos disseminated through the *Wall Street Journal*. They create a Photo Pessimism index using machine learning techniques for large-scale photo classification. The algorithm learns the traits that separate pessimistic and optimistic mood extremes and outputs the probability that a photo is negative. The resulting index of photos negatively predicts the next day's market returns and positively predicts returns for the remaining week.

Sports competitions, TV shows, and music have a transitory impact on social mood. However, stronger, more pervasive emotions may occur in society. A seasonal optimism occurs in Muslim countries during the month-long period of Ramadan. Ramadan is a time for fasting, worship, social awareness, reflection, giving, and a closer relationship with fellow Muslims. Białkowski et al. (2012) show that over 19 years in 14 Muslim countries, Ramadan is associated with an average return of just over 3 percent. The other 11 months average nearly 4 percent in total. Thus, the one month of Ramadan represents about 40 percent of the annual return.

Herding

One mechanism by which social interaction can affect stock prices is through herding. From the investment perspective, *herding* is when groups of investors buy or sell a security on the market over the same period. Nofsinger and Sias (1999) discuss how herding can push prices toward or away from their fundamental values. Herding on information and signals of value moves prices toward their fundamental value. Herding on sentiment moves prices beyond fundament value into bubbles.

Herding research covers several decades. Much of the early literature focused on herding by institutional investors (Sias, 2004), security analysts (Welch, 2000), and mutual funds (Wermers, 1999), and on herding within industries (Choi and Sias, 2009). Researchers often characterize herding as informational cascades (Bikhchandani et al., 1992), in which investors observe the trades of others and follow with similar trades. Recently, studies have examined the herding and sentiment of individual investors through the trading platform Robinhood and in meme stock GameStop (Barber et al., 2022; Welch, 2022). Robinhood investors often concentrate their trading on a few attention-grabbing stocks. Although the trading increases stock prices for the day, returns are negative for the following month. Thus, sentiment is the basis for this type of herding.

Summary and conclusions

People form beliefs through conversations with others. Social interaction conveys information, and emotional content moves them to act within the social norms. As a social mood propagates through society, that pessimistic or optimistic sentiment can move prices through investors herding into or out of securities.

References

Akçay, Erol, and David Hirshleifer. 2021. "Social Finance as Cultural Evolution, Transmission Bias, and Market Dynamics." *PNAS* 118:26, 1–9.

Baker, Malcolm, and Jeffrey Wurgler. 2006. "Investor Sentiment and the Cross-Section of Stock Returns." *Journal of Finance* 61:4, 1645–1680.

Barber, Brad M., Xing Huang, Terrance Odean, and Christopher Schwarz. 2022. "Attention Induced Trading and Returns: Evidence from Robinhood Users." *Journal of Finance* 77:6, 3141–3190.

Białkowski, Jędrzej, Ahmad Etebari, and Tomasz Piortr Wisniewski. 2012. "Fast Profits: Investor Sentiment and Stock Returns during Ramadan." *Journal of Banking and Finance* 36:3, 835–845.

Bikhchandani, Sushil, David Hershleifer, and Ivo Welch. 1992. "A Theory of Fads, Fashion, Custom, and Cultural Change as Informational Cascades." *Journal of Political Economy* 100:5, 992–1026.

Chang, Shao-Chi, Sheng-Syan Chen, Robin K. Chou, and Yueh-Hsiang Lin. 2012. "Local Sports Sentiment and Returns of Locally Headquartered Stocks: A Firm-Level Analysis." *Journal of Empirical Finance* 19:3, 309–318.

Choi, Nicole, and Richard W. Sias. 2009. "Institutional Industry Herding." *Journal of Financial Economics* 94:3, 469–491.

Duflo, Esther, and Emmanuel Saez. 2002. "Participation and Investment Decisions in a Retirement Plan: The Influence of Colleagues' Choices." *Journal of Public Economics* 85:1, 121–148.

Duflo, Esther, and Emmanuel Saez. 2003. "The Role of Information and Social Interactions in Retirement Plan Decisions: Evidence from a Randomized Experiment." *Quarterly Journal of Economics* 118:3, 815–841.

Edmans, Alex, Adrian Fernandez-Perez, Alexandre Garel, and Ivan Indriawan. 2022. "Music Sentiment and Stock Returns around the World." *Journal of Financial Economics* 145:2, 234–254.

Edmans, Alex, Diego Garcia, and Oyvind Norli. 2007. "Sports Sentiment and Stock Returns." *Journal of Finance* 62:4, 1967–1998.

Egan, Daniel, Christoph Merkle, and Martin Weber. 2014. "Second-Order Beliefs and the Individual Investor." *Journal of Economic Behavior and Organization* 107:Part B, 652–666.

García, Diego. 2013. "Sentiment during Recessions." *Journal of Finance* 68:3, 1267–1300.

Hales, Jeffrey, Xi (Jason) Kuang, and Shankar Venkataraman. 2011. "Who Believes the Hype? An Experimental Examination of How Language Affects Investor Judgments." *Journal of Accounting Research* 49:1, 223–255.

Hirshleifer, David. 2015. "Behavioral Finance." *Annual Review of Financial Economics* 7:December, 133–159.

Hirshleifer, David. 2020. "Presidential Address: Social Transmission Bias in Economics and Finance." *Journal of Finance* 75:4, 1779–1831.

Hong, Harrison, Jeffrey D. Kubik, and Jeremy C. Stein. 2004. "Social Interaction and Stock-Market Participation." *Journal of Finance* 59:1, 137–163.

Ivković, Zoran, and Scott Weisbenner. 2007. "Information Diffusion Effects in Individual Investor's Common Stock Purchases: Covet Thy Neighbors' Investment Choices." *Review of Financial Studies* 20:4, 1327–1357.

Kuchler, Theresa, and Johannes Stroebel. 2021. "Social Finance." *Annual Review of Financial Economics* 13:November, 37–55.

Lee, Charles M.C., Andrei Shleifer, and Richard H. Thaler. 1991. "Investor Sentiment and the Closed-End Fund Puzzle." *Journal of Finance* 46:1, 75–109.

Lepori, Gabriele M. 2015. "Investor Mood and Demand for Stocks: Evidence from Popular TV Series Finales." *Journal of Economic Psychology* 48:June, 33–47.

Nofsinger, John R. 2005. "Social Mood and Financial Economics." *Journal of Behavioral Finance* 6:3, 144–160.

Nofsinger, John R., and Richard W. Sias. 1999. "Herding and Feedback Trading by Institutional and Individual Investors." *Journal of Finance* 54:6, 2263–2295.

Obaid, Khaled, and Kuntara Pukthuanthong. 2022. "A Picture Is Worth a Thousand Words: Measuring Investor Sentiment by Combining Machine Learning and Photos from News." *Journal of Financial Economics* 144:1, 273–297.

Pool, Veronika K., Noah Stoffman, and Scott E. Yonker. 2015. "The People in Your Neighborhood: Social Interactions and Mutual Fund Portfolios." *Journal of Finance* 70:6, 2679–2731.

Rantala, Ville. 2019. "How Do Investment Ideas Spread through Social Interaction? Evidence from a Ponzi Scheme." *Journal of Finance* 74:5, 2349–2389.

Shefrin, Hersh. 2005. *A Behavioral Approach to Asset Pricing.* Boston, MA: Academic Press.

Shiller, Robert J. 2017. "Narrative Economics." *American Economic Review* 107:4, 967–1004.

Shiller, Robert J., and John Pound. 1989. "Survey Evidence on Diffusion of Interest and Information among Investors." *Journal of Economic Behavior and Organization* 12:1, 47–66.

Sias, Richard W. 2004. "Institutional Herding." *Review of Financial Studies* 17:1, 165–206.

Siikanen, Milla, Kęstutis Baltakys, Juho Kanniainen, Ravi Vatrapu, Raghava Mukkamala, and Abid Hussain. 2018. "Facebook Drives Behavior of Passive Households in Stock Markets." *Finance Research Letters* 27:December, 208–213.

Welch, Ivo. 2000. "Herding among Security Analysts." *Journal of Financial Economics* 58:3, 369–396.

Welch, Ivo. 2022. "The Wisdom of the Robinhood Crowd." *Journal of Finance* 77:3, 1489–1527.
Wermers, Russ. 1999. "Mutual Fund Herding and the Impact on Stock Prices." *Journal of Finance* 54:2, 581–622.

7 Choice architecture and nudging

Nudges influence behavior by changing the environment in which decisions are made, without restricting the menu of options and without altering financial incentives.
–John Beshears and Harry Kosowsky (2020, p. 3)

Introduction

The framing of a question can affect someone's answer or decision. A simple example is the decision frame of opting in versus opting out. Sometimes, a person must consent to be an organ donor by opting into a program when getting a driver's license. By contrast, an organization may automatically enroll that person in an organ donor program, requiring that individual to opt out if desired. The number of organ donors is much higher in opt-out situations. In either case, a person has the freedom to become an organ donor. Is framing decisions appropriate to nudge people into making good choices? Thaler and Sunstein (2008) contend that the answer should be "yes." Many refer to nudge design as choice architecture.

Decision frames

Different frames can influence the answer to a question. For example, someone can frame a question negatively (the number of people who died) or positively (the number of people who survived). People make different choices when faced with positive versus negative frames. Even the order of presenting information can matter. Nobel laureate Daniel Kahneman (Tversky and Kahneman, 1974) shows that when given ten seconds to estimate the answer to a multiplication problem, the average estimates for $8 \times 7 \times 6 \times 5 \times 4 \times 3 \times 2$ are four times larger than the average estimates for $2 \times 3 \times 4 \times 5 \times 6 \times 7 \times 8$. The only difference between the two problems is the order of presenting the numbers. However, starting with an 8 leads to much higher estimates than beginning with 2. This phenomenon refers to the *framing effect*.

Consider how someone can frame a question in finance. What level do you estimate the S&P 500 Index will be at the end of this year? A slight change in the question is: What return do you estimate the S&P 500 Index will provide from now to the end of this year? The first asks for a price change forecast, while the second asks for a return forecast. Both are the same prediction because converting a level change into a percentage change and vice versa is easy. However, people respond differently when predicting price versus return trends. Glaser et al. (2007) demonstrate that people forecasting a price-level trend predict a slowing or even reversal of a trend that one can consider a mean reversion. *Mean reversion* is when prices revert to the long-term average level. On the other hand, people forecasting a return trend make predictions by extrapolating the trend, a representativeness bias. *Representativeness bias* refers to the mistake of believing two similar things are more closely related than they are. In this case, someone deems the future trend will be similar to the past trend. This frame bias is particularly troubling in finance because of the prevalence of forecasts. For example, analysts estimate prices and earnings, and numerous surveys ask participants about stock and stock market predictions.

Framing is also important in finance when it involves risk and return. *Asset pricing theory* is a fundamental finance theory stating that risk is positively related to expected return. Specifically, a return risk premium should occur when someone takes an additional *systematic risk*, that is, the general risk in the stock market. Thus, the higher the risk taken, the higher the return expected.

Kaustia et al. (2009) consider financial debt an indicator of firm risk. A firm that uses more debt in its capital structure uses financial leverage. The leverage is risky because it magnifies profits when business is good and losses when business is poor. Kaustia et al. surveyed Finnish financial advisors and asked them about the return in two different frames. The researchers asked one set of advisors about the risk premium demanded for firms with high leverage. *A risk premium* is a reward for taking a risk. The total return, including the risk premium, depends on the risk level taken. Investors should require a risk premium if an advisor believes that high debt is a risk factor. Over 85 percent of the advisors responded that highly leveraged firms need a high premium. The total expected return would also increase for high-risk firms with a high-risk premium. The researchers asked other advisors about returns using a different frame. Specifically, the researchers inquired if firms with high debt levels would earn high, low, or the same returns as firms without high leverage. About 12 percent believed higher leverage firms would earn a higher return this time. This example illustrates a negative risk–return relationship, contrary to financial theory and the advisors' answers from the first frame. Thus, decision frames can profoundly affect the decisions people make.

Choice architecture

Choice architecture refers to the specific design of a question or decision. Consider survey questions. Determining what participants believe requires designing questions that are as unbiased as possible. An extreme example involves a *political push poll*, an interactive marketing technique in which an individual or organization attempts to influence prospective voters' views under the guise of conducting an opinion poll. Hence, the pollster designs the questions to elicit an emotional response supporting a particular candidate or issue, thus pushing respondents in a specific political direction. Nudging is a type of choice architecture that attempts to push the participants to make an optimal decision for themselves when they do not know their preferences or they are unclear.

Nudging

Behavioral biases, like cognitive errors and mental shortcuts, influence decisions. These biases can cause people to make poor decisions, especially in the areas of retirement plan contributions and portfolio asset allocation. How can people make better decisions? Should someone help them to make better decisions? Some advocate a maximization of liberty; therefore, the freedom of choice is of the highest value. Others support paternalism, in which an authoritative figurehead, like a government or corporation, makes decisions that benefit others.

Thaler and Sunstein (2008) suggest combining individual choice and paternalism. Specifically, private and public organizations should attempt to guide people's decisions in a direction that improves their welfare while allowing them the freedom to make that choice. Exploiting psychological biases can change people's decisions on eating healthier food, becoming an organ donor, quitting smoking, paying taxes, and improving energy efficiency, as well as those in many other areas.

Save More Tomorrow

The Save More Tomorrow (SMT) program aims to nudge people to contribute more to their retirement plans and make better investment decisions. Instead of setting up a 401(k)-plan enrollment process where social and psychological influences inhibit employees from contributing, SMT's design uses one's biases to encourage employees to contribute.

Before SMT, Madrian and Shea (2001) show that simple decision frame changes could significantly impact defined contribution retirement plans. All plans used to be opt-in. Employees could decide to enroll in their employers' plans at any time. Unfortunately, this approach resulted in status quo bias, causing many employees to procrastinate so long in making their retirement plan decisions that they never complete the paperwork to participate in the plan. *Status quo bias* is a cognitive bias that involves a preference for things to stay the same. Madrian and Shea's research revealed that enrolling employees automatically in a retirement plan and requiring them to act to disenroll (an opt-out design) increased the number of people participating in the program. This result occurred because status quo bias delays the opt-out action. Many eventually stay in the plan. The automatic enrollment comes with a default contribution level (usually 3 percent) and a default asset allocation. One criticism is that most employees stay at the default levels. Some might have participated without the automatic enrollment, contributed a higher amount (i.e., over 3 percent), or chosen a more aggressive asset allocation. Status quo bias might harm these people if they do not change from the defaults to their preferences.

Thaler and Benartzi (2004) propose a four-step SMT approach to help people start contributing to their 401(k) plans or help them increase their contributions. Those not contributing to their plan can agree to begin an SMT program.

- The first step is for an employee to agree to the plan well before the initial contribution so that the decision has no immediate ramifications. One reason people do not enroll in a pension plan is that they are loss-averse and do not want to lose income. *Loss aversion* is the tendency to prefer avoiding losses to acquiring equal gains. The purpose of the delay in the first step is to minimize loss aversion. The first step also implements *present bias*, favoring a smaller current reward to a larger future reward. However, the preference changes to the larger future reward by delaying current and future rewards. Thus, more people will likely enroll by delaying their initial contributions.
- The second step starts with employees agreeing to a small initial contribution rate, such as 2 percent, at their next pay raise. Starting the contribution at the same time as a pay raise shows no negative ramifications because the employee still experiences a slight pay increase. Again, this step minimizes loss aversion.
- The third step is the agreement to increase the contribution rate at each pay raise until it reaches the maximum level.
- The fourth step is that the employee can opt out of the plan at any time. This step makes the employee more comfortable about joining the program, but the hope is that status quo bias works toward them not opting out.

A midsize manufacturing company experiencing low participation in their 401(k) plan implemented SMT. Management asked employees to increase their contribution by 5 percent. The firm offered the SMT program to employees who claimed they could not contribute the 5 percent. The effect of joining the program was dramatic.

- Nearly 80 percent of the employees offered the program accepted.
- After three pay raises, those who had joined had increased their savings rate from 3.5 to 11.6 percent.
- Those who did not join increased their savings rate from 5.3 to 7.5 percent.

The firm has tweaked its SMT's characteristics since its introduction. For example, framing the delayed enrollment option in an SMT process as occurring right after a "fresh start" can impact its effectiveness in influencing people to enroll in the retirement plan. Beshears et al. (2021)

report that mailings describing the future retirement plan savings opportunity as occurring shortly after a fresh start date, like after someone's next birthday, increased take-up of the future savings opportunity compared to (1) mailings that described the opportunity without a temporal landmark, such as two months, and (2) mailings that linked the opportunity to "control" temporal landmarks, like Thanksgiving, Martin Luther King Day, or Valentine's Day.

Lottery-linked savings

The SMT program's success spawned other nudging programs, including Save and Win. This program encourages lower-income households to save more. Many low-income families in the United States believe they are more likely to become rich from lotteries than from saving. Hence, these households frequently participate in lotteries. Save and Win is a savings product with a lottery prize component to encourage more savers and savings. Each savings account deposit or bond purchase includes a "buy-in" to a regular lottery drawing. The savings account earns a slightly lower interest rate than available elsewhere, but the excitement of gambling draws people to start saving. The bank uses the cost savings from paying a lower interest for the lottery prizes. This structure appeals to loss-averse savers because they do not see any losses from gambling, yet they get the excitement of a potential lottery win.

Several credit unions implemented a program called "Save to Win." Participants earned a chance to win monthly cash prizes for each $25 deposit into a savings account. They also accumulated chances to win an annual $100,000 grand prize.

Do such programs promote gambling? Cookson (2018) studies the program to assess whether increased gambling offsets the improved savings rates. The study investigated gambling tendencies by comparing casino cash withdrawals from bank accounts in counties with the new accounts versus casino cash withdrawals from bank accounts in nearby counties without the new accounts. The study suggests that lottery-linked savings plans reduce consumer gambling. The program's lottery activity substitutes for other forms of gambling.

Social influences

The social environment can have a strong influence on decisions. Knowledge of what peers are doing nudges a person into action. Therefore, why not include peer pressure as a commitment device in the choice architecture?

Kast et al. (2018) report on the results of a program's results to give low-income entrepreneurs in Chile the opportunity to increase savings. The researchers randomly assigned the entrepreneurs to three groups. They offered the first group – the control group – a basic savings account. They also offered the second group – the peer group – a basic savings account. However, members of this group could announce their savings goals to their peer group and receive recognition for their progress in weekly meetings. Thus, peer group members experienced social interaction. The researchers offered members of the third group a high interest rate savings account, where the rate was much higher than that of the basic savings account.

What were the results? The entrepreneurs in the peer group (group 2) made 3.7 times more deposits and had almost twice the savings balance than the control group (group 1). The peer group also outperformed the high interest rate group (group 3) because the high interest rate group had a similar savings pattern to the control group. Offering higher interest rates did not improve savings. However, adding a peer pressure aspect to the choice architecture did enhance savings. This program combined two elements of social influence: peer pressure and an aspirational effect of seeing one's social group members' success.

The researchers divided the peer group to disentangle these two social influences and replaced face-to-face meetings. Instead, one subgroup received informational messages about the saving of others in the group – the aspirational effect. The researchers assigned participants in the second subgroup a Savings Buddy from which they received updates about each other – the peer pressure effect. The two groups had similar savings patterns. Thus, peer pressure and aspirational effects are effective in nudging programs.

A national pension system reform in Israel is another example of where social influence had an impact. Before the reform, all employees contributed to an investment fund chosen by the employer. The reform allowed employees to select any of over 200 prominent funds for their plan. Choosing from more than 200 funds can overwhelm many people. Who changed from the original investment fund to one or more new funds, and why? Mugerman et al. (2014) report that the status quo bias led most people to keep their existing funds. Their evidence shows that 93 percent did not switch funds.

What motivated the other 7 percent to pick a new fund? They did not base their decisions on investment characteristics like low management fees or performance. However, peer effects had an impact. The researchers report that where employees work in the same department the choices of colleagues in that department influence an individual's fund choice. The association is even stronger between the fund selected and the funds chosen by coworkers in the same ethnic group. In other words, the people with whom an employee is most likely to socialize had a more significant impact on their fund choice than fund investment characteristics.

Nudge legitimacy

Does using choice architecture to persuade people to choose desired results make them better off? One concern about nudging is the side effects, indirect outcomes, or unintended consequences. Given that indirect ramifications are under-studied, should public policy use nudging?

Side effects

Choice architecture implementation and evaluation studies focus on the direct effects of a specific behavior of interest. Little regard exists for the potential indirect effects. For example, as demonstrated, nudges can increase savings via automatic enrollment or contribution escalation. However, what happens to the rest of the household budget? What is the source of the additional money invested – consumption or debt? Does automatic enrollment trigger more borrowing and potential financial distress?

Beshears et al. (2022) examine this question. Before August 2010, civilian Army employees had to opt into contributing to the Thrift Savings Plan (TSP), the defined contribution plan of the U.S. federal government. Starting on August 1, 2010, the Army automatically enrolled new employees in the TSP at a default contribution rate of 3 percent of their income. The study finds that automatic enrollment increased cumulative employer plus employee contributions as intended up to four years later. Fortunately, the study reveals little evidence of increased financial distress. The automatic enrollment caused no significant change in debt stress measures like credit scores, debt balances, excluding auto loans and mortgages, or late balances or balances in collection. Thus, the nudging increased pension contributions without the negative indirect effect of causing credit distress.

On the other hand, Medina (2021) studies the direct and indirect effects of a simple nudge of sending a reminder about an upcoming credit card payment due. The researcher experimented in Brazil, where the credit card late payment fee was 14 percent, and a checking account overdraft fee was 9 percent. The reminder of the upcoming credit card bill caused a decrease in credit card late payments as intended. However, overdraft charges in checking accounts increased for users with a history of overdrawing their accounts. These users experienced a net increase of 5 percent in total fees. People without a history of overdrafts experienced a saving of 15 percent. This nudge led to unintended net adverse effects for those facing liquidity constraints.

Public policy

Considerable debate exists about whether nudging violates sound public policy principles requiring transparency, acknowledgment of citizen preferences, and a reasonable degree of informed decision-making. Ridder et al. (2022), in their literature review, find that transparency does not compromise nudge effects because participants are equally responsive to nudges regardless of whether someone discloses their presence, purpose, or working mechanisms. They also report that nudges are generally ineffective when they do not match preexisting preferences of goals and intentions. If a person does not want to contribute to a retirement plan, rather than simply feels unable to do so, nudging will not cause that person to enroll. Nudges have the most significant effect when people have less developed preferences because they doubt their choice. Lastly, Ridder et al. show that nudges are less effective when people use intuitive thinking processes, which should have made them more susceptible to nudge influence. The authors conclude that these three criticisms are moderately important at best.

Summary and conclusions

Behavioral biases affect how people interpret the information given in a question. Thus, the decision frame profoundly influences their assessment of the situation and the decision reached. Poorly designed choice architecture influences people to make suboptimal decisions due to biases. However, governments and companies can design many financial programs to nudge people toward making good choices for their welfare. Many still hotly debate whether these entities should use nudges.

References

Beshears, John, James J. Choi, David Laibson, Brigitte C. Madrian, and William L. Skimmyhorn. 2022. "Borrowing to Save? The Impact of Automatic Enrollment on Debt." *Journal of Finance* 77:1, 403–447.

Beshears, John, Hengchen Dai, Katherine L. Milkman, and Shlomo Benartzi, 2021. "Using Fresh Starts to Nudge Increased Retirement Savings." *Organizational Behavior and Human Decision Processes* 167, 72–87.

Beshears, John, and Harry Kosowsky. 2020. "Nudging: Progress to Date and Future Directions." *Organizational Behavior and Human Decision Processes* 161, 3–19.

Cookson, J. Anthony. 2018. "When Saving Is Gambling." *Journal of Financial Economics* 129, 24–45.

Glaser, Markus, Thomas Langer, Jens Reynolds, and Martin Weber. 2007. "Framing Effects in Stock Market Forecasts: The Difference between Asking for Prices and Asking for Returns." *Review of Finance* 11:2, 325–357.

Kast, Felipe, Stephan Meier, and Dina Pomeranz. 2018. "Saving More in Groups: Field Experimental Evidence from Chile." *Journal of Development Economics* 133, 275–294.

Kaustia, Markku, Heidi Laukkanen, and Vesa Puttonen. 2009. "Should Good Stocks Have High Prices or High Returns?" *Financial Analysts Journal* 65:3, 55–62.

Madrian, Brigitte, and Dennis Shea. 2001. "The Power of Suggestion: Inertia in 401(k) Participation and Savings Behavior." *Quarterly Journal of Economics* 116:4, 1149–1187.

Medina, Paolina C. 2021. "Side Effects of Nudging: Evidence from a Randomized Intervention in the Credit Card Market." *Review of Financial Studies* 34:5, 2580–2607.

Mugerman, Yevgeny, Orly Sade, and Moses Shayo. 2014. "Long Term Savings Decisions: Financial Reform, Peer Effects and Ethnicity," *Journal of Economic Behavior and Organization* 106, 235–253.

Ridder, Denise de, Floor Kroese, and Laurens van Gestel. 2022. "Nudgeability: Mapping Conditions of Susceptibility to Nudge Influence." *Perspectives on Psychological Science* 17:2, 346–359.

Thaler, Richard H., and Shlomo Benartzi. 2004. "Save More Tomorrow: Using Behavioral Economics to Increase Employee Savings." *Journal of Political Economy* 112:S1, S164–S187.

Thaler, Richard H., and Cass R. Sunstein. 2008. *Nudge: Improving Decisions about Health, Wealth, and Happiness.* New Haven, CT: Yale University Press.

Tversky, Amos, and Daniel Kahneman. 1974. "Judgment under Uncertainty: Heuristics and Biases." *Science* 185:4157, 1124–1131.

8   The psychology of retirement

> *When you enter retirement, there are three important unknowns. You have no idea what investment returns are going to be in retirement. You also don't know how long you're going to live. And you don't know how much you're going to have to spend.*
>
> –Michael Finke (Carly Schulaka, 2016, pp. 16–17)

Introduction

Retirement decisions require intense, long-term planning and the ability to manage complex financial instruments such as annuities and 401(k) retirement plans. Individuals envision retirement as a special and rewarding time when they take vacations and no longer deal with the daily pressures of their careers. However, this dream of an enjoyable retirement experience is at risk for many people because they have not saved enough money, made bad investment decisions, and failed to plan for retirement. This chapter discusses retirement biases and research findings on specific retirement products.

Maintaining the status quo

The most prevalent bias suffered by retirement savers is *status quo bias*, as discussed in Chapter 7. This bias occurs when people accept the current situation because of procrastination or prefer to keep things the same. Individuals trying to change the psychology of inertia require strong motivation. They fail to adjust their financial strategies despite knowing that change is beneficial. Employees delay contributing to their retirement plans or postpone pursuing a financial professional's advice to learn about different retirement choices. After beginning to allocate funds for a company retirement plan, most employees do not actively oversee their accounts.

Agnew et al. (2003) examine 7,000 retirement accounts between April 1994 and August 1998. Their findings reveal that most people in their sample fail to diversify across asset classes. Many invest 100 percent of their investments in stocks. These retirement savers exhibit status quo bias regarding their asset allocation choices. They do not change their allocation after the initial allocation decision. As evidence, the authors report low portfolio turnover rates and minimal account rebalancing.

Mitchell et al. (2006) study over 1,500 company 401(k) plans with 1.2 million accounts. Their findings reveal that during a two-year period most retirement savers suffer from inertia, with most 401(k) savers not executing any trades.

Retirement biases

Individuals suffer from biases during the retirement planning process. The following discusses different biases, illustrates each, and suggests steps to overcome them.

Representativeness

As discussed in Chapter 3, *representativeness* proposes that people are inclined to make judgments based on the similarity of items or predict future uncertain events by taking a small portion of data and drawing a general subjective conclusion. For example, an individual purchased a life insurance policy with high premiums but eventually canceled it due to its cost. As a result of this bias, the person concludes that all life insurance policies are too expensive. In this case, a financial planner should present the client with an affordable policy meeting the client's comfort level. Over time the financial planner may recommend that the client consider increasing the amount of life insurance.

Overconfidence or hubris

Many people suffering from *overconfidence* overestimate their skills and predictions for future success. They suffer from hubris, defined as excessive self-confidence or pride. Such individuals are usually aggressive risk-takers or short-term thinkers, ignore relevant warning signs, and fail to develop contingency plans. Overconfident people often consider life insurance unnecessary because they overestimate their life expectancies. At a minimum, a financial professional can suggest that this client take advantage of an employer's low-cost term life insurance, if available.

Negative affect

Negative affect focuses on negative emotions, like worry, fear, and stress. Gino et al. (2012) report that individuals experiencing anxiety are more likely to seek and rely on advice. Anxious people have difficulty distinguishing between good and bad financial advice about various retirement services and products. The lesson for ensuring a more positive outcome is to make complex and critical financial decisions in a quiet, less stressful environment.

Framing

Framing is a cognitive bias where people decide on options based on whether the presentation has positive or negative connotations, as discussed in Chapter 7. A person viewing life insurance as "death insurance" discounts its value. Reframing life insurance as potential retirement income or a source of funds for long-term care may lessen this negative connotation.

Affect heuristic

The *affect heuristic* is a mental shortcut allowing individuals to make judgments and solve issues quickly and efficiently by using feelings or emotions. For example, after a relative's death, family and friends collect money to pay for the funeral since the deceased had no life insurance and little savings. A client overreacts to this event by wanting to purchase the maximum affordable amount of life insurance. A financial planner can encourage the client to take out an appropriate amount of life insurance as part of a comprehensive financial plan and mitigate the client's emotional response.

Retirement plans and income

This section discusses the psychological aspects of 401(k) plans, individual retirement accounts (IRAs), annuities, and Social Security benefits.

401(k) plans

A major U.S. retirement plan for a company's employees is a 401(k) plan. Extensive research reveals that 401(k) participants suffer from several biases resulting in inferior mutual fund selection and investment underperformance of their accounts. One study examines if mutual fund families that are service providers for 401(k) plans exhibit favoritism toward their specific affiliated mutual funds. Pool et al. (2016, p. 1779) conclude, "Using a hand-collected data set on the menu of investment options offered to plan participants ... fund deletions and additions are less sensitive to prior performance for affiliated than unaffiliated funds." The authors also find no evidence that retirement savers reverse this affiliation bias with their investment selections. This finding also might be associated with retirement participants' status quo bias.

Doellman et al. (2019) investigate whether the names of mutual funds appearing in alphabetical order for 401(k) plans influence participants' investment allocation choices. The findings reveal that it does, and the impact increases as the number of funds in the plan increases. This bias is strong even when few funds are available in the plan menu.

Other research evidence concerns how men and women make investment and savings decisions. Morrin et al. (2011) studies the gender effects on participation in retirement plans and mutual fund assortment size within 401(k) plans. *Assortment size* refers to the number of funds offered in a plan. The findings demonstrate that larger mutual fund assortments decrease plan participation for females but increase it for males. Bailey et al. (2004) show that males contribute more to 401(k) plans than their female counterparts.

Some retirement savers engage in excessive trading because of overconfident behavior. Tang (2016) examines the accounts of over one million momentum traders in 401(k) plans. These traders sell the outperforming funds and chase past investment returns resulting in poor yearly performance. The study's findings reveal that momentum traders might earn negative returns of up to 2.1 percent annually. Choi et al. (2002) examine the trading behavior and investment performance for 18 months within a 401(k) savings online platform. The trading rate doubled for participants with online access (e.g., web-based systems) compared to a control group without online access. Online traders tend to make smaller trades and possess investment portfolios with lower market values than those without online access. The authors find no evidence that any new trading on the Web is successful.

Benartzi (2001) examines the relationship between excessive extrapolation bias and employee company stock ownership within a 401(k) plan. *Extrapolation bias* is the inclination to overweight recent stock performance and expect it to continue. The study's findings reveal that employees of companies that recorded the top stock returns over the past ten years allotted nearly 40 percent of their voluntary contributions to the firm's equity stock, whereas workers of firms with the lowest equity returns allocated about 10 percent of their optional contributions to their company's stock.

Agnew et al. (2012) evaluate the role of trust and knowledge about the retirement plan as variables for 401(k) participation. The authors report that within a discretionary enrollment environment, demographic factors and plan knowledge are connected to 401(k) plan participation. For automatic enrollment situations, participation is linked with trust in financial organizations and plan knowledge of the available retirement plan.

Kronlund et al. (2021) investigate the influence of new regulatory reform in 2012 that required disclosures of investment performance and fees for the different investment options within a 401(k) plan. The authors reveal that retirement participants are considerably more aware of short-term investment returns and expense ratios following the reform enactment. The impact of disclosure was higher for plans with substantial average contributions per client account and lower for plans with numerous investment choices. Kronlund et al. (2021, p. 644) conclude that the "findings suggest that providing salient fee and performance information can mitigate participants' inertia in retirement plans."

Another trend with 401(k) plans is using nudging, whereby a company automatically enrolls its employees into its retirement plan, as discussed in Chapter 7. Nudging reveals how governments, nonprofits, or companies can create strategies or programs that affect decisions (Thaler and Sunstein, 2009). This policy aims to increase employee retirement participation and contributions in 401(k) plans.

Individual retirement accounts

An individual retirement account (IRA) is another plan used by many savers. An *IRA* is a tax-favored personal savings arrangement allowing someone to set aside money for retirement. It is popular among employees who do not have a company retirement plan within their workplace, since they can open this type of account individually. The degree of financial literacy and the emotional mood of retirement savers influence their willingness to invest in an IRA.

Chatterjee (2010) reports that individuals with higher levels of educational attainment are more likely to have IRAs. Schooley and Worden (2013) reveal that education, investment knowledge, and self-discipline toward finances increase the chances of contributing to an IRA. Financial distress (negative affect) decreases the chances of contributing additional money to an IRA. Bernstein (2004) reports that households highly dependent on debt, such as credit cards, have a lower likelihood of opening an IRA than households using credit for a mortgage loan. The author also finds that most households starting to save within an IRA view retirement as less important than other financial planning goals, such as refinancing mortgage debt or paying down outstanding balances on credit card loans.

About 50 percent of the workforce lacks company-sponsored retirement plans, increasing the chances that these workers will not have retirement savings (Belbase and Sanzenbacher, 2017). Recently, local jurisdictions started to offer IRA programs requiring companies to use automatic enrollment of their workers into a state-sponsored IRA. For employees without company plans, Belbase and Sanzenbacher (2017) examine the influence of auto-enrollment on the probability of participation in state-sponsored IRAs. Their findings show that workers without a company retirement plan, or "uncovered workers," have a high probability of opening and contributing to these state-sponsored IRAs (public sector) at comparable rates compared to employees auto-enrolled into company-sponsored 401(k) plans (private sector). The findings also reveal that participants automatically enrolled in these plans start to opt out voluntarily when the auto-escalation contribution rate exceeds 6 percent. *Auto-escalation* is a retirement plan strategy that involuntarily increases the contribution payment at a regular fixed period up to a predetermined maximum rate.

Research evidence demonstrates that financial professionals influence retirement savers regarding IRA participation. Frischmann et al. (1998) report that tax experts paid by individuals to complete their returns are more likely to increase the participation rates within IRAs among these taxpayers. Shen and Turner (2018) examine the legitimacy of the claim among financial experts that transferring a 401(k) plan from a previous employer into an IRA is worthwhile since the former has a limited choice of investment selections unlike the IRA with unrestricted financial choices. The authors reveal that financial professionals with a "conflict of interest" might use "strategic complexity to encourage rollovers, recommending complex portfolios to impress naïve clients who have a weak understanding of the concept of diversification" (Shen and Turner, 2018, p. 47). These two studies demonstrate that expert financial advice can sometimes have favorable or unfavorable consequences for clients.

An emerging area of research in retirement planning deals with the *theory of planned behavior* (TPB), a theory of psychology that connects beliefs to behavior. This theory has three major elements – attitude, subjective norms, and perceived behavioral control – that collectively form a person's behavioral goals. Magwegwe and Lim (2021, p. 116) developed a model based on TPB wherein behavioral factors affect the computation of "retirement savings needs" which in turn influences IRA ownership. The authors find that favorable attitudes, strong social norms, and perceived behavioral control are associated with calculating retirement savings needs. Factors influencing the forecast of IRA ownership include determining savings needs for retirement, feeling in psychological control, and using an employer's retirement plan.

Annuities

Annuities are a critical aspect of retirement planning since they promise guaranteed fixed monthly income for an individual during retirement. Annuities are financed years in advance, with a lump sum or a series of regular payments. However, many research studies report that retirement savers and retirees fail to understand the advantages of, or are unwilling to invest in, annuity products. At retirement age, individuals can decide whether to accept their 401(k) account balance as a lump sum distribution or convert the lump sum into a series of annuity payments, known as the *process of annuitization*. Only a small percentage of retirees decide to annuitize their retirement investments (i.e., convert their lump sum retirement savings to a guaranteed stream of payments to ensure lifetime income) or invest in the annuity. This is called the *annuitization or annuity puzzle* (Benartzi et al., 2011).

In a rational world, the premise is that more retirees should annuitize their investments because this strategy guarantees they will potentially have a lifetime of income and not outlive their retirement savings, thus eliminating longevity risk. *Longevity risk* is when someone outlives retirement savings and then only has Social Security as a source of income. Panis (2004) reports that retirees owning annuities or having guaranteed fixed payments within a pension plan have higher satisfaction levels during retirement.

Schreiber and Weber (2016) examine the annuitization puzzle and disclose that older individuals are more predisposed to select the lump sum distribution than younger individuals. The authors report that hyperbolic discounting is the main reason for the low rate of annuitization. *Hyperbolic discounting* is when individuals select smaller, rapid rewards instead of bigger, future rewards. This phenomenon happens more often when the delay is closer to the present day than the distant future.

Chen et al. (2019) investigate whether cumulative prospect theory, as related to loss aversion, can explain why individuals express a low preference for immediate annuities. An *immediate annuity* is a lump sum amount converted today into a continuing, fixed income stream for a specified time that might end before death. The study shows that loss aversion is a significant reason for retirees not purchasing immediate annuities. This loss-averse behavior is associated with concern about experiencing the regret of buying an immediate annuity. Also, many individuals do not want to relinquish personal control of managing a sizeable 401(k) investment portfolio. They also lack trust in distributing the proceeds in a lump sum to an insurance company.

In contrast, Olsen's (2007) research proposes that annuities might be a strategy for overcoming loss-averse behavior for some people. The evidence suggests that certain investor types might be inclined to find specific attributes of annuities pleasing, such as the certainty of payment dates and fixed income amounts. Olsen proposes that individuals who suffer from loss aversion make judgments based on emotion. If they want to reduce biases connected with regret and control, they may find certain features of annuities attractive. Another characteristic that individuals find appealing for investing in annuities is the payment structure. Beshears et al. (2014) report that most individuals prefer one higher monthly bonus payment each year combined with marginally decreased payments for the remaining 11 months.

When presented as incremental choices, individuals increase their willingness to buy deferred annuities or annuitize their investment accounts. Beshears et al. (2014) report that annuitization increases among respondents when the framing of the annuity choice is a portion or percentage of their overall wealth instead of an "all or nothing" selection. Bockweg et al. (2018) also report this finding. Specifically, they show that participants in a Dutch pension fund view a partial lump sum option as more appealing than mandatory full annuitization. Shu et al. (2016, p. 241) find that in "annuities with the same expected payout but different annual increases and period certain guarantees, the proportion of consumers who choose the annuity over self-management can vary by more than a factor of 2."

Agnew et al. (2008) find that women are more likely to invest in an annuity than men, even after controlling for risk tolerance and financial knowledge. The authors also report that individuals with higher risk aversion and financial literacy levels are more likely to invest in an annuity product. Furthermore, Goedde-Menke et al. (2014) disclose that most individuals have low "annuity literacy," especially respondents unfamiliar with an annuity's essential features. This finding demonstrates the importance of educating retail clients about annuities, enabling them to make better-informed judgments and assess this financial product's appropriateness.

Social Security benefits

Most Americans claim Social Security benefits before full retirement age at the detriment of their long-term financial wealth. Many retirees claim these benefits when they become eligible at 62 and only receive about 70 percent of their full retirement benefits if they had waited until 67. For example, if the full benefit at 67 is $2,500 per month, the retiree who claims it at 62 would only receive $1,750 per month. The $2,500 per month payment is the rational choice since claiming Social Security benefits at a full retirement age of 67 provides much higher payments and wealth if a person lives into their early 80s or longer. The $1,750 per month is an emotional selection since people enjoy receiving the payment today and do not have the self-control to wait until a full retirement age of 67.

Most Americans do not understand or realize that the Social Security program has many attributes of an annuity product. As previously mentioned, most individuals avoid converting their private investment savings, such as a 401(k) plan, from a lump sum to a series of annuity payments. However, when presented with a monthly payment at age 62 from a government program, most retirees elect this option. They fail to see a connection between an annuity insurance product from the private sector and an annuity government product from the public sector. In terms of the private investment portfolio lump sum, savers exhibit a high internal locus of control and do not want to surrender this personal control of their investments. However, when claiming Social Security benefits at 62, individuals suffer from a lack of self-control. This situation demonstrates the different types of control that can negatively influence retirement decisions.

Psychological biases, such as loss aversion and framing effects, influence Social Security claiming decisions. Guo et al. (2020) apply prospect theory (i.e., based on loss aversion in which a loss feels twice as bad as a gain feels good) as a potential explanation for individuals claiming Social Security benefits early. The authors disclose that when people evaluate claiming benefits, they contemplate benefit gains versus losses in postponing claiming compared to receiving benefits instantly. Respondents suffer from loss aversion because "fear of receiving less lifetime benefits in the event of early death induces them to claim immediately" (Guo et al. 2020, p. 490).

Brown et al. (2016) examine whether framing influences an individual's judgments about taking Social Security benefits. The study reports that subjects are more likely to postpone receiving benefits when framing future claiming as a gain, and that the "claiming age" is a reference point or anchor at more advanced ages. Also, the framing effect influences people with outstanding credit card debt, lower financial literacy, and lower income than other cohorts.

The uncertainty about the financial strength of the Social Security system affects how workers perceive the amount they will receive in future benefits. Turner and Rajnes (2021) assess employees' expectations about their future benefits from Social Security over time. The authors evaluate data from more than 60 individual survey iterations conducted between 1971 and 2020, with a sample size exceeding 130,000. Many employees expect to be paid Social Security benefits at retirement age, but the outlook on the payment amounts is highly pessimistic. Most workers expect to receive benefits below what they are entitled to because of the current financial problems associated with the Social Security program.

Delavande and Rohwedder (2011) examine whether people experiencing high uncertainty toward receiving future benefits payments are influenced by that uncertainty when making current investment decisions regarding planning for retirement. The authors report that individuals who exhibit high uncertainty toward future expected Social Security payments own a smaller percentage of overall wealth in stock investments. Therefore, this feeling of uncertainty is potentially causing retirement savers to have a lower risk tolerance toward riskier assets such as common stocks.

An approach to better understanding why individuals elect to claim Social Security before retirement age is to collect qualitative information using research methods such as interviews or focus groups. Rabinovich and Samek (2018) examine how Americans of retirement age think about how and when they should claim Social Security payments with a focus group of 68 retirees. Most individuals collected their benefits early; in particular, about 45 percent elected for payments at 62. Most participants express satisfaction with electing to claim benefits early since they base their decisions on such factors as the need for income to pay daily living expenses, their mortality, and concerns over the Social Security program's financial strength. Others suggest they might have claimed Social Security closer to retirement age under different circumstances, such as having more money saved or other sources of income in retirement. This evidence suggests that claiming Social Security benefits is a multi-dimensional decision based on a retiree's financial situation.

Another critical aspect of the research literature examines the role of mental and physical health behaviors and their connection to claiming Social Security benefits. DeSimone (2018) reports a 7 to 8 percent decline in the U.S. suicide rate when reaching 62. DeSimone (2018, p. 435) proposes that the most likely reason for this finding is "Social Security early retirement benefit eligibility rather than retirement per se."

Knoll et al. (2018) reveal that the increase in obesity and therefore of obesity-related illnesses influences how people evaluate claiming Social Security benefits. This situation might result in smaller monthly payments and lower total retirement benefits during the lifetime of people with these types of health issues. The authors also report that this situation could have a more significant financial effect on individuals with a lower socioeconomic status than on other groups.

Summary and conclusions

Retirement is a complex and overwhelming issue for many retirement savers and retirees. Understanding the various biases associated with complex financial products such as 401(k) plans, IRAs, annuities, and Social Security benefits may result in better retirement outcomes. A strong planning relationship and a good communication channel between financial professionals and their clients are essential to ensure clients experience satisfaction during their retirement years.

References

Agnew, Julie R., Lisa R. Anderson, Jeffrey R. Gerlach, and Lisa R. Szykman. 2008. "Who Chooses Annuities? An Experimental Investigation of the Role of Gender, Framing, and Defaults." *American Economic Review* 98:2, 418–422.
Agnew, Julie, Pierluigi Balduzzi, and Annika Sunden. 2003. "Portfolio Choice and Trading in a Large 401(k) Plan." *American Economic Review* 93:1, 193–215.

Agnew, Julie R., Lisa R. Szykman, Stephen P. Utkus, and Jean A. Young. 2012. "Trust, Plan Knowledge and 401(k) Savings Behavior." *Journal of Pension Economics and Finance* 11:1, 1–20.

Bailey, Jeffrey J., John R. Nofsinger, and Michele O'Neill. 2004. "401(K) Retirement Plan Contribution Decision Factors: The Role of Social Norms." *Journal of Business and Management* 9:4, 327–344.

Belbase, Anek, and Geoffrey T. Sanzenbacher. 2017. "Default Contribution Rates and Participation in Automatic IRAs by Uncovered Workers." *Geneva Papers on Risk and Insurance: Issues and Practice* 42:3, 376–388.

Benartzi, Shlomo. 2001. "Excessive Extrapolation and the Allocation of 401(k) Accounts to Company Stock." *Journal of Finance* 56:5, 1747–1764.

Benartzi, Shlomo, Alessandro Previtero, and Richard H. Thaler. 2011. "Annuitization Puzzles." *Journal of Economic Perspectives* 25:4, 143–164.

Bernstein, David. 2004. "Household Debt and IRAs: Evidence from the Survey of Consumer Finances." *Financial Counseling and Planning* 15:1, 63–72.

Beshears, John, James J. Choi, David Laibson, Brigitte C. Madrian, and Stephen P. Zeldes. 2014. "What Makes Annuitization More Appealing?" *Journal of Public Economics* 116:August, 2–16.

Bockweg, Christian, Eduard Ponds, Onno Steenbeek, and Joyce Vonken. 2018. "Framing and the Annuitization Decision – Experimental Evidence from a Dutch Pension Fund." *Journal of Pension Economics and Finance* 17:3, 385–417.

Brown, Jeffrey R., Arie Kapteyn, and Olivia S. Mitchell. 2016. "Framing and Claiming: How Information-Framing Affects Expected Social Security Claiming Behavior." *Journal of Risk and Insurance* 83:1, 139–162.

Chatterjee, Swarn. 2010. "Retirement Savings of Private and Public Sector Employees: A Comparative Study." *Journal of Applied Business Research* 26:6, 95–102.

Chen, Anran, Steven Haberman, and Stephen Thomas. 2019. "Cumulative Prospect Theory and Deferred Annuities." *Review of Behavioral Finance* 11:3, 277–293.

Choi, James J., David Laibson, and Andrew Metrick. 2002. "How Does the Internet Affect Trading? Evidence from Investor Behavior in 401(k) Plans." *Journal of Financial Economics* 64:3, 397–421.

Delavande, Adeline, and Susann Rohwedder. 2011. "Individuals' Uncertainty about Future Social Security Benefits and Portfolio Choice." *Journal of Applied Econometrics* 26:3, 498–519.

DeSimone, Jeffrey. 2018. "Suicide and the Social Security Early Retirement Age." *Contemporary Economic Policy* 36:3, 435–450.

Doellman, Thomas W., Jennifer Itzkowitz, Jesse Itzkowitz, and Sabuhi H. Sardarli. 2019. "Alphabeticity Bias in 401(k) Investing." *Financial Review* 54:4, 643–677.

Frischmann, Peter J., Sanjay Gupta, and Gary J. Weber. 1998. "New Evidence on Participation in Individual Retirement Accounts." *Journal of the American Taxation Association* 20:2, 57–82.

Gino, Francesca, Alison Wood Brooks, and Maurice E. Schweitzer. 2012. "Anxiety, Advice, and the Ability to Discern: Feeling Anxious Motivates Individuals to Seek and Use Advice." *Journal of Personality and Social Psychology* 102:3, 497–504.

Goedde-Menke, Michael, Moritz Lehmensiek-Starke, and Sven Nolte. 2014. "An Empirical Test of Competing Hypotheses for the Annuity Puzzle." *Journal of Economic Psychology* 43:August, 75–91.

Guo, Rui, Wei Sun, Jianqiu Wang, and Gang Xiao. 2020. "Why Do Retired Workers Claim Their Social Security Benefits So Early? A Potential Explanation Based on the Cumulative Prospect Theory." *Applied Economics* 52:5, 490–505.

Knoll, Melissa A. Z., Dave Shoffner, and Samantha O'Leary. 2018. "The Potential Effects of Obesity on Social Security Claiming Behavior and Retirement Benefits." *Journals of Gerontology: Series B, Psychological Sciences and Social Sciences* 73:4, 723–732.

Kronlund, Mathias, Veronika K. Pool, Clemens Sialm, and Irina Stefanescu. 2021. "Out of Sight No More? The Effect of Fee Disclosures on 401(k) Investment Allocations." *Journal of Financial Economics* 141:2, 644–668.

Magwegwe, Frank M., and HanNa Lim. 2021. "Factors Associated with the Ownership of Individual Retirement Accounts (IRAs): Applying the Theory of Planned Behavior." *Financial Counseling and Planning* 32:1, 116–130.

Mitchell, Olivia S., Gary R. Mottola, Stephen P. Utkus, and Takeshi Yamaguchi. 2006. "The Inattentive Participant: Portfolio Trading Behavior in 401(k) Plans." Working Paper No. 2006-115, University of Michigan.

Morrin, Maureen, Susan Broniarczyk, and J. Jeffrey Inman. 2011. "Fund Assortments, Gender, and Retirement Plan Participation." *International Journal of Bank Marketing* 29:5, 433–450.

Olsen, Robert A. 2007. "Investors' Predisposition for Annuities: A Psychological Perspective." *Journal of Financial Service Professionals* 61:5, 51–57.

Panis, Constantijn W. A. 2004. "Annuities and Retirement Well-Being." In Olivia S. Mitchell and Stephen P. Utkus (eds.), *Pension Design and Structure: New Lessons from Behavioral Finance*, 259–274, Oxford: Oxford University Press.

Pool, Veronika K., Clemens Sialm, and Irina Stefanescu. 2016. "It Pays to Set the Menu: Mutual Fund Investment Options in 401(k) Plans." *Journal of Finance* 71:4, 1779–1812.

Rabinovich, Lila, and Anya Samek. 2018. "'No Regrets': Qualitative Evidence on Early Claiming of Social Security Retirement." *Journal of Aging Studies* 46:September, 17–23.

Schooley, Diane K., and Debra Drecnik Worden. 2013. "Accumulating and Spending Retirement Assets: A Behavioral Finance Explanation." *Financial Services Review* 22:2, 173–186.

Schreiber, Philipp, and Martin Weber. 2016. "Time Inconsistent Preferences and the Annuitization Decision." *Journal of Economic Behavior and Organization* 129:September, 37–55.

Schulaka, Carly. 2016. "Michael Finke on the Truth about Retirement Spending, the Annuity Puzzle, and Changing the Paradigm." *Journal of Financial Planning* 29:10, 14–19.

Shen, Sally, and John A. Turner. 2018. "Conflicted Advice about Portfolio Diversification." *Financial Services Review* 27:1, 47–81.

Shu, Suzanne B., Robert Zeithammer, and John W. Payne. 2016. "Consumer Preferences for Annuity Attributes: Beyond Net Present Value." *Journal of Marketing Research* 53:2, 240–262.

Tang, Ning. 2016. "The Overlooked Momentum Traders in 401(k) Plans." *Financial Services Review* 25:1, 51–72.

Thaler, Richard H., and Cass R. Sunstein. 2009. *Nudge: Improving Decisions about Health, Wealth, and Happiness*. New York: Penguin Books.

Turner, John A., and David Rajnes. 2021. "Workers' Expectations about Their Future Social Security Benefits: How Realistic Are They?" *Social Security Bulletin* 81:4, 1–17.

9 Behavioral corporate finance

Theories from behavioral finance are at the forefront of explaining differences in corporate financial policies and capital structures. Most important, however, behavioral corporate finance has reintroduced humanity – in all its complexity and subtlety – into corporate finance, where indeed it belongs.
–David E. Adler (2004)

Introduction

Much early academic work in behavioral finance took a market perspective, focusing on market anomalies, market efficiency, and speculative behavior. Other research examined individual investor investment decisions, especially in relation to risks, heuristics, and behavioral biases. Attention eventually turned to *corporate finance*, the acquisition and allocation of corporate funds or resources to achieve an objective, such as maximizing shareholder value. Thus, corporate finance relates to company decisions that have a financial or monetary impact.

In line with standard finance, which has been discussed earlier in the book, standard corporate finance assumes perfectly rational managers and efficient markets. It focuses on what corporate managers should do: make rational financial decisions and act in shareholders' best interests. By contrast, behavioral corporate finance (BCF) deals with what people actually do. Consequently, it often challenges conventional ideas about corporate finance. *BCF* is a subdiscipline of corporate finance that integrates psychology and economics into studying human judgment and decision-making biases under uncertain conditions within corporations. Thus, it investigates how people behave in corporations to understand them better and suggests how they might improve their decision-making.

Unlike standard finance, BCF assumes that markets are not always efficient and that corporate executives are not always rational. It views financial executives as ordinary people who make judgments and decisions about risky alternatives. Their decision-making is imperfect because they are sometimes emotional, illogical, and impulsive. They are also subject to behavioral biases such as overconfidence or extreme optimism that can cloud their decision-making and reduce corporate value. Additionally, corporate managers may exhibit behavioral errors in analyzing, interpreting, and presenting data. According to Baker et al. (2007), BCF replaces traditional rationality assumptions with potentially more realistic behavioral assumptions. Consequently, BCF's underlying assumptions require reexamining conventional ideas about corporate finance.

Paths of behavioral corporate finance

Baker et al. (2007) identify two primary paths of BCF investigation. One involves examining corporate finance transactions when corporate managers exhibit behavioral biases. The other concerns how rational managers make decisions about security mispricing when investors are not entirely rational.

Irrational managers

Like shareholders, corporate managers can also exhibit irrational behavior. Two situations in which managers exhibit irrationality involve overconfidence and loss aversion.

Overconfidence

Overconfidence is the tendency to overestimate one's abilities. This bias occurs when a person's subjective confidence in their judgments exceeds the objective accuracy of those judgments. Overconfident individuals believe they know more than they do. They overestimate their knowledge, skills, and information relative to others, especially if they have strong past performance (Daniel et al., 1998; Odean, 1998). Numerous factors may influence the degree of overconfidence, like gender, culture, and the amount of information, monetary incentives, and expertise (Glaser and Weber, 2010). Researchers use many other proxies for overconfidence, like self-attribution bias (Daniel et al., 1998) and unrealistic optimism (Glaser and Weber, 2007). *Self-attribution bias* is when people attribute successful outcomes to their actions and bad outcomes to external factors, leading to underperformance (Heider, 1958). Psychologists view people as unrealistically optimistic if they predict that a future personal outcome will be more favorable than a relevant, objective standard suggests.

Being a victim of this ego or superiority trap can severely affect corporate decision-making and performance. For example, Ben-David et al. (2013) find that having overconfident financial executives leads to miscalibration when making estimates or setting overly optimistic expectations. The authors also report that companies with overconfident chief financial officers (CFOs) follow more aggressive corporate policies, like applying lower discount rates to value cash flows, investing more, and using more debt. CFOs are also less inclined to pay dividends, more likely to repurchase shares, and use proportionally more long-term versus short-term debt. Additionally, overconfident managers may only incorporate new information slowly because they are self-assured in their initial decisions. As discussed later in this chapter, a link exists between chief executive officer (CEO) overconfidence and dividend policy. Additionally, excessively optimistic and overconfident executives are more likely to engage in acquisitions and overpay for them.

Loss Aversion

As discussed in Chapter 1, *loss aversion* is the tendency to prefer avoiding losses to acquiring equivalent gains. People often feel the pain of a loss more strongly than the pleasure of an equal gain. Thus, avoiding a $20 million loss is better than gaining $20 million. This bias can lead to bad financial decisions. Individuals, including corporate managers, may give greater weight to potential costs and failures than possible benefits and rewards in their decision-making.

By prioritizing avoiding losses over earning gains, corporate managers avoid financial risks and make overly conservative decisions that affect a firm's potential growth. For instance, when making capital budgeting decisions, they may favor "safe" investments over innovative but more risky ones with higher return potential but a greater chance of a loss. Corporate managers may focus on current products and services instead of introducing new ones or entering new markets. Loss aversion could prevent senior managers from making the best decisions for their companies to avoid failure or risk. Loss aversion could also lead them to hold on to capital projects that have declined in value to avoid realizing a loss, even when selling or abandoning a project is prudent.

Rational managers and irrational investors

Corporate managers can act rationally even if their company's shareholders do not. One example concerns market timing and corporate financial structure. Standard corporate finance theory indicates firms should follow a target capital structure to maximize shareholder wealth. However, evidence suggests that companies time their equity issues to exploit positive investor sentiment and market mispricing (Baker and Wurgler, 2000, 2002). This chapter discusses other examples of the decisions of rational managers and irrational investors.

Four pillars of corporate policy decisions

This section examines behavioral concepts that are mainly associated with the four pillars of corporate policy decisions.

- *Capital budgeting* and other investment decisions. What long-term investments should a firm choose?
- *Capital structure/financing decisions.* How should a firm finance its investments?
- *Dividend policy decisions.* Should a firm distribute funds to its shareholders, and if so, how?
- *Working capital management.* How should a firm manage and finance its current assets and current liabilities?

Later sections review related BCF topics regarding corporate governance, initial public offerings (IPOs), and mergers and acquisitions (M&As).

Capital budgeting decisions

Capital budgeting is a firm's process of evaluating potential major projects or investments. It includes identifying potential projects, forecasting their future cash flows, determining a project's appropriate discount rate, establishing decision criteria for project adoption and termination, and implementing projects. Capital budgeting is important because it often involves substantial outlays that ultimately determine a firm's profitability, value, and viability (Gervais, 2010).

Corporate managers encounter challenges at each stage of the capital budgeting process, as illustrated by many projects exceeding their budgets, taking longer than planned, and failing to meet expectations. Shefrin (2018) attributes these failings to the *planning fallacy*, where managers fail to adjust for past overconfidence and excessive optimism when making plans. Overconfidence and excessive optimism are related but distinct psychological biases. According to Dowling and Lucey (2010, pp. 320–321), "Overconfidence involves placing too much weight on the accuracy of private information and an excessive belief in personal skills. Excessive optimism follows from overconfidence and involves a belief that future events are more likely to be positive than is realistic."

Corporate managers may suffer from overconfidence, leading to understating project risk and the discount rate used in capital budgeting decisions. Overconfident managers also underestimate a project's cost but overestimate its value. Their overconfidence may stem from various behavioral biases, such as the *illusion of control bias*, which is the tendency to overstate one's degree of control or influence over external events. Although corporate executives have control over their capital budgeting decisions, they lack control over the outcomes resulting from those decisions. They are also prone to psychologically induced excessive optimism, resulting in biased probabilities and overstating a project's cash flows due to anchoring on the forecasts of those proposing the project. Overconfidence and excessive optimism lead corporate managers to overinvest, prompting capital budgeting mistakes.

Corporate managers often use theoretically correct discounted cash flow (DCF) techniques, like net present value (NPV) and internal rate of return (IRR), to determine which proposed fixed assets to accept or reject (Graham and Harvey, 2001). However, their analysis is only as sound as the quality of the inputs, which are subject to biases. Other firms use less sound project adoption criteria, such as the *payback method*, referring to the time required to recoup the funds expended in an investment.

Why would these corporate executives rely on the payback rather than NPV or IRR? Several biases explain this choice. One reason is that payback is the most intuitive of the three capital budgeting techniques. Thus, comfort is important to some financial managers. Capital budgeting decisions involve objective and subjective factors. Some executives prefer making subjective judgments rather than relying on objective measures. Shefrin (2018, p. 99) notes, "… avoiding DCF and NPV analysis means that capital budgeting decisions involve subjective judgment. And subjective judgment leads managers to be vulnerable to behavioral biases." Finally, some executives prefer to depend on the *affect heuristic*, which describes how people rely on their emotional reactions or feelings when making decisions (Slovic, 2000).

Although corporate managers sometimes must decide whether to terminate a project, they may be reluctant to abandon failing projects, despite that being the rational choice. Instead, they may delay the decision or put more money into a failed project, called the *escalation of commitment*. Shefrin (2018) offers several reasons for refusing to terminate failing projects. First, corporate managers try to avoid losses due to *loss aversion*. A sure loss is psychologically painful. Second, they may have *regret aversion bias*. Regret aversion is a concept within prospect theory (Kahneman and Tversky, 1979) describing a negative emotional bias that urges people to avoid regret associated with poor decision-making. Corporate managers want to avoid admitting that they made a wrong choice that was costly to their firm. Since they are regret-averse, they favor the status quo. *Status quo bias* is the preference to leave things the way they are over changing them. Third, corporate managers have *confirmation bias*, the tendency to search for, interpret, favor, and recall information confirming or supporting prior beliefs or values. Thus, they overweight information confirming their views and underweight information disconfirming them.

Capital structure/financing decisions

The traditional approach to capital structure offers several theories. Modigliani and Miller (1958), who conducted the first study on capital structure theory, assert that a firm's capital structure does not affect its value, implying the irrelevance of debt policy. Modigliani and Miller (1963) later revised their theory to include taxes, contending that debt increases firm value due to interest tax shields, up to a point where the cost of financial distress outweighs the benefits from interest tax shields. They refer to this notion as the trade-off theory. Myers and Majluf (1984) set forth the pecking order theory, which contends that firms have a preferred order of preference when raising capital because of the threat of providing a wrong signal to the market. Firms prefer using cash from retained earnings (internal equity), followed by debt and external equity. Since Modigliani and Miller's seminal work, many studies have attempted to explain how firms choose their capital structure and whether an optimal one exists.

Shefrin (2018) identifies five elements affecting capital structure: (1) tax shields, (2) expected costs of financial distress, (3) signaling stemming from asymmetric information, (4) management discipline, and (5) financial flexibility. Assuming rational managers and efficient markets, managers make financing decisions to balance these five elements (Shefrin, 2018). However, traditional theories neglect the effect of the decision-maker's personality and psychological biases on the capital structure decision. Thus, capital structure decisions and financial behavior may deviate from the traditional paradigm. In practice, traditional and behavioral considerations drive financing decisions (Gider and Hackbarth, 2010). Still, managerial biases regarding financing decisions do not necessarily result in decisions consistent with investor preferences (Bilgehan, 2014).

One popular stream of the BCF literature focuses on how managerial traits of overconfidence and excessive optimism affect capital structure decisions. Overconfident managers believe that the market undervalues their firms and that the risk of debt is lower than that of equity. They tend to choose higher debt levels relative to their rational counterparts, leading to excessive leverage and a higher probability of financial distress (Esghaier, 2017).

Dividend policy decisions

Dividend policy refers to how much in dividends a company pays its shareholders and the frequency of such payments. According to standard finance theory, dividend policy involves a trade-off between reducing the cost of retaining excess cash and lowering the cost of external financing for future investment when corporate decision-makers act in the interest of existing shareholders. As an alternative to paying cash dividends, a *share repurchase* is when a company purchases its shares from the marketplace. It represents a more flexible way of returning money to shareholders because repurchases tend to be less regular than cash dividends. Since cash dividends and share repurchases are not psychologically equivalent, managers view them differently.

Standard finance offers various theories about dividend payout decisions, like bird-in-hand theory, residual dividend theory, clientele theory, the asymmetric information and signaling approach, and an agency explanation. Baker et al. (2011, p. 251) conclude, "There is no clear winner among the competing dividend theories, and no single theory has become the dominant solution to the dividend puzzle." The *dividend puzzle* refers to why companies pay dividends and investors want them (Black, 1976).

A behavior-based approach emerged with Kahneman and Tversky (1979), who focused on identifying various biases of economic agents. Several behavioral explanations help to understand the dividend puzzle (Ben-David, 2010).

Managerial Emotional Biases and Dividend Policy

Various studies empirically link managerial emotional biases (i.e., overconfidence, excessive optimism, and loss aversion) and dividend policy. Ali and Anis (2012) provide survey evidence from Tunisian companies' CEOs. The authors find that leaders who are overconfident and/or optimistic about their companies' future investment opportunities tend to distribute dividends to signal firm performance and enjoy a positive market reaction. CEO loss aversion also correlates with the dividend payment. Their concern with losing remuneration or reputation limits using risky external financing like debt. Therefore, they prefer preserving the cash flow by reducing dividend payments.

Deshmukh et al. (2013) assert that overconfident CEOs view external financing as costly and build financial slack for future investment needs by lowering the current dividend payout. Their evidence shows the level of dividend payout is about one-sixth lower in firms managed by overconfident CEOs. The authors also document that the dividend reduction associated with CEO overconfidence is greater in firms with lower growth opportunities and lower cash flow.

Self-Control Theory

Shefrin and Statman (1984) offer behavioral explanations of dividend policy based on self-control theory (Thaler and Shefrin, 1981) and prospect theory (Kahneman and Tversky, 1979). They examine why individual investors find cash dividends attractive. Individuals are often unable to delay gratification because of a lack of self-control. The authors contend investors do not treat receiving dividends and generating cash from a stock sale as perfect substitutes. Instead, they adjust their consumption to the level of dividends received, substituting the discipline of a firm's dividend policy for their lack of self-control if they need to sell shares of stock to finance consumption. That is, these investors consume dividends but avoid dipping into capital. According to Shefrin and Statman, some investors are willing to pay a premium for cash dividends because of self-control reasons, the desire to segregate, or the wish to avoid regret, despite potentially higher tax payments on dividends.

Catering Theory of Dividends

Baker and Wurgler (2004) propose a *catering theory* of dividends in which the prevailing investor demand for dividend payers drives the decision to pay dividends. It assumes that some investors are uninformed. Catering theory states that when investors' dividend demand changes, the market prices of dividend-paying and non-paying firms also change. The difference in firms' market value according to the choice of consumers for dividend payment is called the *dividend premium*.

Managers cater to investor demand by paying dividends when investors put a stock price premium on dividend-paying firms and by not paying when investors prefer non-dividend firms. Baker and Wurgler (2004) contend that an optimistic investor's time-varying demand relates to dividend sentiment. When the dividend premium is high, investors seek companies that exhibit safety characteristics, and when it is low, they seek maximum capital growth. Assessing this prediction reveals that nonpayers initiate dividends when demand is high, and payers omit dividends when demand is low. Empirical evidence on the catering theory of dividends is mixed (de Rooji and Renneboog, 2009).

Why set a catering dividend policy to meet investor needs? This policy could affect a stock's short-term price and behavioral-adjusted present value (BPV) but not its intrinsic value. BPV is the sum of V_L and aV_S, where V_L is the stock's value to long-term investors, V_S is the stock's value to short-term investors, and a is a non-negative weighting parameter reflecting the importance to managers of V_S relative to V_L. Shefrin (2018, p. 190) provides the following example of catering and price effects.

> Consider how paying an extra dollar of dividends might impact a firm. First, costs relate to taxes and financing, which enter through V_L. When maximizing BPV, managers need to be sure that they can compensate for these costs through benefits associated with incremental V_S. These benefits come from generating a higher stock price and market timing activity to exploit possible overvaluation.

Firm Life-Cycle Theory of Dividends

Several researchers propose a life-cycle theory of dividends, such as Mueller (1972), Damodaran (1999), and Lease et al. (2000). However, Lease et al.'s competing frictions model excludes behavioral considerations. A firm's pattern of dividends changes as a function of a firm's life cycle: start-up, IPO, rapid growth, maturity, and decline. As a firm matures, its ability to generate cash exceeds its ability to identify profitable investment opportunities. Eventually, distributing dividends to shareholders becomes appropriate. Thus, a firm does not usually start paying cash dividends until maturity. It increases its dividends or repurchases stock during the declining stages. Bulan and Subramanian (2009, p. 211) conclude, "Overall, the empirical evidence favors the firm life cycle theory of dividends in terms of dividend payment propensity and life cycle characteristics."

Behavioral Signaling

Managers tend to smooth dividend payments to limit reducing those payouts because doing so often produces adverse price effects (Brav et al., 2005). Some firms establish a dividend policy regarding dividends per share (DPS), which serves as a reference point. Over time they seek to stabilize or smooth DPS by making occasional increases but avoiding decreases and omissions unless necessary. This dividend policy is called *behavioral signaling*. According to Shefrin (2018), managers attempt to maximize BPV in markets where their investors use reference points associated with consumption to measure gains and losses. Managers consider loss aversion where investor reaction to losses relative to their reference points is greater than equivalent gains. They want shareholders to construe dividend payout policy as a signal to increase the stock price.

Garrett and Priestley (2000) propose a behavioral model of dividend policy where managers adjust dividends toward a target level. Adjusting dividends and deviating from the target dividend involve costs. Managers optimize by setting dividends to minimize these costs.

Behavioral Preference Patterns

Breuer et al. (2014) investigate the relevance of behavioral determinants for corporate dividend policies across 29 countries. Their determinants of investor dividend preferences are ambiguity aversion, loss aversion, and patience. Their findings link loss aversion and ambiguity aversion to dividend policies. Specifically, they find that investors with higher ambiguity aversion prefer higher dividend ratios, and that the general dividend level increases with greater loss aversion. The authors also find that more patient investors prefer lower dividends than impatient investors do. Like the catering theory, the authors contend that managers try to satisfy their investors' preferences.

Working capital management

The fourth pillar of corporate finance policy – *working capital management* (WCM) – concerns the decision-making process involving different components of working capital, such as cash, accounts receivable, inventory, accounts payable, and risk management. *Working capital* is the money available to meet a firm's short-term obligations. Its purpose is to ensure a company's efficient operation by monitoring and using its current assets and liabilities effectively. Research in corporate finance focuses on the first three pillars – investment, financing, and dividend decisions – with much less attention paid to WCM. The behavioral aspects of short-term or WCM decisions are under-addressed and require additional attention. However, several survey-based studies examine whether working capital managers are prone to the following heuristic-driven biases.

- *Self-serving bias* is the tendency of people to credit their successes to personal or internal factors but blame their failures on external factors beyond their control.
- *Confidence level bias* is how assured individuals are about the reliability of their knowledge, skills, qualifications, and expertise.
- *Loss aversion bias* is the tendency to prefer avoiding losses to acquiring equivalent gains.

- *Anchoring* or *representativeness bias* is the tendency to rely too heavily on a particular reference point or anchor, such as the first piece of information received on a topic.
- *Representativeness bias* is a long-run anchoring bias that bases judgments on stereotypes, trends, and patterns.

The following studies show that working capital managers exhibit behavioral biases when making WCM decisions. Ramiah et al. (2014) examine whether Australian corporate treasurers exhibit specific biases. The empirical results show they are prone to self-serving, high confidence level, loss aversion, and anchoring biases that affect various WCM areas. For example, highly confident managers rely heavily on their estimation models and forecasting techniques. However, the authors note that behavioral biases are not necessarily bad attributes because they can potentially enhance managerial decisions in certain areas. For instance, managers with loss aversion bias tend to manage bad debt more efficiently. Their findings imply that firms should know their WCM goals and hire candidates with behavioral biases to help achieve them.

Three other studies examine the same four behavioral factors related to WCM but in different countries: Iqbal and Butt (2015) and Haider and Siddiqui (2020) in Pakistan, and Bellouma (2016) in Tunisia. These studies find that behavioral variables – self-serving, confidence level, loss aversion, and anchoring or representativeness – affect WCM. Bellouma concludes that firms can use psychological attributes to draw a specific profile for working capital managers based on the financial situation. For example, companies under financial distress should hire managers with representativeness and loss aversion biases to reduce risk-taking, control debt, and monitor doubtful customers. However, companies in more favorable scenarios should seek more confident working capital managers with a self-serving bias.

Corporate governance

A corporation's board of directors has several responsibilities, like recruiting, supervising, retaining, evaluating, and compensating managers and executives. According to traditional finance, the board should ensure that a CEO's interests match those of a firm and its shareholders. The main goal is value maximization resulting from an increase in a firm's share prices. Supposedly, the board can accomplish this goal with properly designed incentives such as stock options because they encourage the CEO to seek increases in the share price. However, if a CEO exhibits persistent biases or a particular leadership style, such incentives may not align with the parties' interests. For example, Shefrin (2018, p. 222) notes, "The combination of aspiration-based risk-taking and overconfidence can also induce ambitious, unethical managers to manipulate accounting information in order to exercise their stock options when the stock is over priced."

By contrast, behavioral finance research suggests that traditional corporate governance views may be overly simplistic. According to Shefrin (2001), limits exist to what incentives can achieve. Thus, the board must look beyond incentive-based compensation to attract a CEO whose background, personality, and style mesh with a firm's challenges.

Initial public offerings

An *initial public offering* (IPO) describes a firm's transition from private to public ownership. It prices a firm's shares and changes its organization, ownership structure, and relation with capital markets. The IPO literature discusses three components of the so-called *IPO puzzle*: initial underpricing (Loughran and Ritter, 1995), the hot-issue market (Ritter, 1984), and long-term underperformance (Ritter, 1991). These IPO anomalies reflect decisions made by financial executives and market participants and raise questions about market efficiency. Researchers have advanced many theories reflecting rational and irrational behavior to help explain the IPO puzzle. Jenkinson and Ljungqvist (2001), Adams et al. (2008), and Derrien (2010) offer detailed reviews of such explanations for underpricing of newly listed companies.

As suggested, a documented phenomenon is IPO underpricing. IPOs often exhibit positive and sizeable first-day returns, indicating the offer price is too low. That is, investment bankers systematically underprice IPOs. Why would issuers leave "money on the table" by voluntarily allowing their initial stock to be underpriced, resulting in a substantial cost to them?

One "rational" explanation is that information asymmetries exist between the various IPO parties – the issuer, its underwriter, and the investors. These asymmetries result in different risks for these parties. If issuing firms are more informed than investors, underpricing is a cost that firms must pay to signal their quality to the market. Thus, the initial underpricing reflects compensation for risk and agency conflicts between different parties.

Another rational explanation involves investment banks engaged in underwriting and providing analyst coverage during the post-IPO period. Issuers may be more concerned with maintaining good relations with investment bankers whose analysts try to create "buzz" about their companies. Thus, they may indirectly pay for analyst coverage by agreeing to initial underpricing (Shefrin, 2018).

Others contend that the IPO puzzle is a manifestation of market inefficiency caused by the irrational behaviors of investors and IPO issuing firms. The highly positive average first-day returns could partially relate to sentiment investors, who tend to be excessively optimistic retail investors. *Investor sentiment* is a belief about future cash flows and investment risks unjustified by the facts. Underwriters allocate most IPO shares to rational institutions, who gradually sell off their shares to sentiment investors, who are overly optimistic about a firm's prospects. These investors may overreact when responding to the hype surrounding an IPO. *Overreaction bias* is the tendency to overreact to new information, creating a larger-than-appropriate effect on a security's price. It is a consequence of having emotion in the market. Thus, retail investors' role is limited to aftermarket trading and may indirectly affect the IPO pricing decision.

Behavioral finance theory offers many other explanations for the underpricing phenomenon (Adams et al., 2008). One reason underwriters underprice new stock is to make share placement easier. Underpricing reduces the chances that the issue will be undersubscribed, resulting in a loss and reputational damage to the underwriters. Because underwriters usually are obligated to prevent a price drop in the aftermarket, this likelihood decreases if an issue is underpriced, not overpriced. This rationale is known as the *price-support explanation of underpricing*. Since underwriters are risk-averse, loss aversion may also influence their pricing behavior. Issuers may accept underpricing if it creates excess demand

and leads to the desired post-IPO structure, such as spreading the stock among numerous stockholders. Another behavioral explanation for IPO underpricing is the underwriter's liability. Investment bankers are concerned with potential lawsuits if an IPO falls below the issue price. Hence, underwriters depress the offer price to limit liability.

Regarding the two other components of the IPO puzzle, firms may issue IPOs in a hot-issue market when the market overvalues firms in their industry. During intense sentiment periods, underwriters set IPO prices above fundamental (intrinsic) value but below the price sentiment investors are willing to pay. Thus, IPOs enable firms and their underwriters to exploit sentiment investors who exhibit excessive optimism and overvalue their stocks. Ritter (1991) refers to this situation as the "window of opportunity" hypothesis. It also helps explain high short-term returns and subsequent price reversals when sentiment demand disappears and stocks return to their fundamental values, resulting in long-run IPO underperformance (Derrien, 2010).

Mergers and acquisitions

The final topic concerns M&As. A *merger* is an agreement uniting two separate entities into one new company, while an *acquisition* refers to the takeover of one entity by another. Two streams of M&A literature are available (Dong, 2010). One assumes that rational bidders and target managers operate in inefficient markets to exploit the misvaluation (Shleifer and Vishny, 2003). The other assumes irrational managers operating in efficient markets. It focuses on the effects of managerial behavioral bias involving M&As (Baker et al., 2007). This section deals with the second of these.

Roll (1986) sets forth the "hubris hypothesis" of takeovers to explain why bidding firms overpay for their targets and thus make a valuation error that, on average, generates no profits. According to the hubris hypothesis, the acquiring firm's management is sometimes over-optimistic in evaluating potential targets because of information asymmetry and misplaced confidence about its ability to make good decisions. Bidding-firm managers hold the unrealistic belief that they can manage the target firm's assets more efficiently than its current management. Overconfident managers overestimate expected gains and underestimate the risk, leading to poor subsequent performance. Thus, the bidder experiences the *winner's curse*, a tendency for the winning bid in an auction to exceed the item's intrinsic value or true worth.

Evidence by Doukas and Petmezas (2007) shows that companies with overconfident managers earn lower merger announcement returns and exhibit poorer long-term share price performance. The authors also find that managerial overconfidence stems from self-attribution bias. Managers with self-attribution bias may become overconfident, leading to underperformance. Specifically, the authors find that when companies engage in many acquisitions they experience lower wealth effects than with initial deals. Thus, managers often credit the initial success to their ability, become overconfident, and engage in more deals. Malmendier and Tate (2008) document that managerial overconfidence partially explains takeover decisions. Additionally, the market reacts negatively when overconfident CEOs make bids.

Summary and conclusions

Traditional corporate finance offers robust theories and techniques enabling managers to make value-maximizing decisions for their firms. It assumes that managers are rational and markets are efficient. In practice, however, managers face psychological pitfalls hampering their ability to apply these theories and techniques. Psychologically induced mistakes can be expensive, detrimental to shareholder interest, and reduce firm value. Thus, corporate managers must be aware of psychological phenomena, such as biases and heuristics, influencing their actions and negatively affecting firm value.

References

Adams, Michael, Barry Thornton, and George Hall. 2008. "IPO Pricing Phenomena: Empirical Evidence of Behavioral Biases." *Journal of Business and Economics Research* 6:4, 67–74.
Adler, David E. 2004. "A Behavioral Theory of Corporate Finance." *Strategy* 34: Spring. Available at https://www.strategy-business.com/article/04113.

Ali, Azouzi Mohamed, and Jarboui Anis. 2012. "CEO Emotional Bias and Dividend Policy: Bayesian Network Method." *Business and Economic Horizons* 7:1, 1–18.

Baker, H. Kent, J. Clay Singleton, and E. Theodore Veit. 2011. *Survey Research in Corporate Finance: Bridging the Gap between Theory and Practice.* Oxford: Oxford University Press.

Baker, Malcolm P., Richard Ruback, and Jeffrey Wurgler. 2007. "Behavioral Corporate Finance: A Survey." In B. Espen Eckbo (ed.), *Handbook of Corporate Finance: Empirical Corporate Finance,* Volume 1, 145–186. Amsterdam: North-Holland.

Baker, Malcolm P., and Jeffrey Wurgler. 2000. "The Equity Share in New Issues and Aggregate Stock Returns." *Journal of Finance* 55:5, 2219–2257.

Baker, Malcolm P., and Jeffrey Wurgler. 2002. "Market Timing and Capital Structure." *Journal of Finance* 57:1, 1–32.

Baker, Malcolm P., and Jeffrey Wurgler. 2004. "A Catering Theory of Dividends." *Journal of Finance* 59:3, 1125–1165.

Bellouma, Meryem. 2016. "Decision-Making of Working Capital Managers: A Behavioral Approach." *Journal of Business Studies Quarterly* 7:4, 30–43.

Ben-David, Itzhak. 2010. "Dividend Policy Decisions." In H. Kent Baker and John R. Nofsinger (eds.), *Behavioral Finance: Investors, Corporations, and Markets,* 435–451. Hoboken, NJ: John Wiley & Sons, Inc.

Ben-David, Itzhak, John R. Graham, and Campbell R. Harvey. 2013. "Managerial Miscalibration." *Quarterly Journal of Economics* 128:4, 1547–1584.

Bilgehan, Tekin. 2014. "Psychological Biases and the Capital Structure Decisions: A Literature Review." *Theoretical and Applied Economics* 21:12, 123–142.

Black, Fischer. 1976. "The Dividend Puzzle." *Journal of Portfolio Management* 2:2, 3–8.

Brav, Alon, John R. Graham, Campbell R. Harvey, and Roni Michaely. 2005. "Payout Policy in the 21st Century." *Journal of Financial Economics* 77:3, 483–572.

Breuer, Wolfgang, Marc Oliver Rieger, and Can Kalender Soypak. 2014. "The Behavioral Foundations of Corporate Dividend Policy: A Cross-Country Analysis." *Journal of Banking and Finance* 42:May, 247–265.

Bulan, Laarni T., and Naryanan Subramanian. 2009. "The Firm Life Cycle Theory of Dividends." In H. Kent Baker (ed.), *Dividends and Dividends Policy,* 201–213. Hoboken, NJ: John Wiley & Sons, Inc.

Damodaran, Aswath. 1999. *Applied Corporate Finance.* New York: John Wiley & Sons, Inc.

Daniel, Kent, David Hirshleifer, and Avanidhar Subrahmanyam, 1998. "Investor Psychology and Security Market Under- and Overreactions." *Journal of Finance,* 53:6, 1839–1885.

de Rooji, Margot, and Luc Renneboog. 2009. "The Catering Theory of Dividends." In H. Kent Baker (ed.) *Dividends and Dividend Policy,* 215–338. Hoboken, NJ: John Wiley & Sons, Inc.

Derrien, François. 2010. "Initial Public Offerings." In H. Kent Baker and John R. Nofsinger (eds.), *Behavioral Finance: Investors, Corporations, and Markets,* 475–490. Hoboken, NJ: John Wiley & Sons, Inc.

Deshmukh, Sanjay, Anand M. Goel, and Keith M. Howe. 2013. "CEO Over-confidence and Dividend Policy." *Journal of Financial Intermediation* 22:3, 440–463.

Dong, Ming. 2010. "Mergers and Acquisitions." In H. Kent Baker and John R. Nofsinger (eds.), *Behavioral Finance: Investors, Corporations, and Markets*, 491–509. Hoboken, NJ: John Wiley & Sons, Inc.

Doukas, John A., and Dimitris Petmezas. 2007. "Acquisitions, Overconfident Managers and Self-Attribution Bias." *European Financial Management* 13:3, 531–577.

Dowling, Michael, and Brian Lucey. 2010. "Other Behavioral Biases." In H. Kent Baker and John R. Nofsinger (eds.), *Behavioral Finance: Investors, Corporations, and Markets*, 313–330. Hoboken, NJ: John Wiley & Sons, Inc.

Esghaier, Ridha. 2017. "Capital Structure Choices and Behavioral Biases: An Application to a Panel of US Industrial Companies." *International Journal of Economics and Financial Issues* 7:4, 608–622.

Garrett, Ian, and Richard Priestley. 2000. "Dividend Behavior and Dividend Signaling." *Journal of Financial and Quantitative Analysis* 35:2, 173–189.

Gervais, Simon. 2010. "Capital Budgeting and Other Investment Decisions." In H. Kent Baker and John R. Nofsinger (eds.), *Behavioral Finance: Investors, Corporations, and Markets*, 413–434. Hoboken, NJ: John Wiley & Sons, Inc.

Gider, Jasmin, and Dirk Hackbarth. 2010. "Financing Decisions." In H. Kent Baker and John R. Nofsinger (eds.), *Behavioral Finance: Investors, Corporations, and Markets*, 393–412. Hoboken, NJ: John Wiley & Sons, Inc.

Glaser, Markus, and Martin Weber. 2007. "Overconfidence and Trading Volume." *Geneva Risk and Insurance Review* 32:1, 1–36.

Glaser, Markus, and Martin Weber. 2010. "Overconfidence." In H. Kent Baker and John R. Nofsinger (eds.), *Behavioral Finance: Investors, Corporations, and Markets*, 241–258. Hoboken, NJ: John Wiley & Sons, Inc.

Graham, John R., and Campbell R. Harvey. 2001. "The Theory and Practice of Corporate Finance: Evidence from the Field." *Journal of Financial Economics* 60:2–3, 187–243.

Haider, Salwa, and Danish Ahmed Siddiqui. 2020. "A Behavioural Finance Approach to Working Capital Management in Context of Pakistani Firms." *International Journal of Scientific and Engineering Research* 11:8, 930–952.

Heider, Fritz. 1958. *The Psychology of Interpersonal Relations*. New York: John Wiley & Sons, Inc.

Iqbal, Sajid, and Safdar Ali Butt. 2016. "Impact of Behavioural Biases on Working Capital Management of Manufacturing Sector of Pakistan: A Non Parametric Investigation Approach." *International Letters of Social and Humanistic Sciences* 55, 147–153.

Jenkinson, Tim J., and Alexander Ljungqvist. 2001. *Going Public: The Theory and Evidence of How Companies Raise Equity Capital*, Second Edition. Oxford and New York: Oxford University Press.

Kahneman, Daniel, and Amos Tversky. 1979. "Prospect Theory: An Analysis of Decision under Risk." *Econometrica* 47:2, 263–291.

Lease, Ronald C., Kose John, Avner Kalay, Uri Loewenstein, and Oded H. Sarig. 2000. *Dividend Policy: Its Impact on Firm Value*. Boston, MA: Harvard Business School Press.

Loughran, Tim, and Jay R. Ritter. 1995. "The New Issue Puzzle." *Journal of Finance* 50:1, 23–51.

Malmendier, Ulrike, and Geoffrey Tate. 2008. "Who Makes Acquisitions? CEO Overconfidence and the Market's Reaction." *Journal of Financial Economics* 89:1, 20–43.

Modigliani, Franco, and Merton H. Miller. 1958. "The Cost of Capital, Corporation Finance, and the Theory of Investment." *American Economic Review* 48:3, 261–297.

Modigliani, Franco, and Merton H. Miller. 1963. "Corporation Income Taxes and the Cost of Capital: A Correction." *American Economic Review* 53:3, 433–443.

Mueller, Dennis C. 1972. "A Life Cycle Theory of the Firm." *Journal of Industrial Economics* 20:3, 199–219.

Myers, Stewart C., and Nicholas S. Majluf. 1984. "Corporate Financing and Investment Decisions When Firms Have Information that Investors Do Not Have." *Journal of Financial Economics* 13:2, 187–221.

Odean, Terrance. 1998. "Are Investors Reluctant to Realize Their Losses?" *Journal of Finance* 53:5, 1775–1798.

Ramiah, Vikash, Yilang Zhao, Imad Moosa, and Michael Graham. 2014. "A Behavioural Finance Approach to Working Capital Management." *European Journal of Finance* 22:8–9, 1–26.

Ritter, Jay R. 1984. "The 'Hot Issue' Market of 1980." *Journal of Business* 57:2, 215–240.

Ritter, Jay R. 1991. "The Long-Run Performance of Initial Public Offerings." *Journal of Finance* 46:1, 3–27.

Roll, Richard. 1986. "The Hubris Hypothesis of Corporate Takeovers." *Journal of Business* 59:2, 197–216.

Shefrin, Hersh. 2001. "Behavioral Corporate Finance." *Journal of Applied Corporate Finance* 14:3, 113–126.

Shefrin, Hersh. 2018. *Behavioral Corporate Finance: Concepts and Cases for Teaching Behavioral Finance*, Second Edition. New York: McGraw-Hill Education.

Shefrin, Hersh M., and Meir Statman. 1984. "Explaining Investor Preference for Cash Dividends." *Journal of Financial Economics* 13:2, 253–282.

Shleifer, Andrei, and Robert W. Vishny. 2003. "Stock Market-Driven Acquisitions." *Journal of Financial Economics* 70:3, 295–311.

Slovic, Paul. 2000. *The Perception of Risk*. London: Earthscan.

Thaler, Richard H., and Hersh M. Shefrin. 1981. "An Economic Theory of Self-Control." *Journal of Political Economy* 89:2, 392–410.

10 Behavioral finance enters its second generation

Behavioral finance seeks to describe the choices not of rational or irrational man, but of real people. The benefits of these insights are already being observed.
–Lucy F. Ackert (2014, p. 39)

Introduction

Dinah Washington won a Grammy Award in 1959 for Best Rhythm and Blues Performance for "What a Diff'rence a Day Makes." The song begins with "What a difference a day makes 24 little hours." Sometimes things change from one day to the next. For behavioral finance, change and acceptance took much longer. Many believers in standard finance once viewed behavioral finance advocates as heretics. The ideas offered by the new finance were controversial, if not shocking, and contradicted conventional wisdom. Traditionalists believed that behavioralists must have made mistakes somewhere. Many viewed the demise of behavioral finance as imminent. That prediction failed to materialize.

Over the decades, behavioral finance evolved, gaining wide acceptance among finance academics and practitioners. The battle was long and hard. Today, behavioral finance is a worthy endeavor that merits attention by adding a human element to the finance discipline. Additionally, observing actual behavior helps in developing good theory. Countless works offer new theories, explanations, and empirical evidence on the financial aspects of human behavior. However, the journey continues.

So far, this book has mainly focused on the foundations of behavioral finance. Statman (2019) describes the first generation of behavioral finance as accepting standard finance's notion that investors focus on the utilitarian benefits of wealth. However, proponents of behavioral finance view people as "predictably irrational" because they engage in shortcuts and errors that mislead them in trying to achieve their rational wants. Ackert (2014, p. 37) states, "Behavioral finance researchers have made great progress in building on this base to provide more satisfactory explanations of observed individual and market behavior."

The second generation

Statman (2017, 2019) believes behavioral finance has entered its second generation. Statman (2019, p. xiv) notes, "Behavioral finance, like all fields of science, is a work in progress, and there are no sharp timelines separating the second generation of behavioral finance from the first." Nonetheless, this transition roughly occurred toward the end of the 20th century.

Behavioral finance provides an alternative for each of the five foundation blocks of standard finance discussed in Chapter 1. Specifically, behavioral finance asserts that:

1. People are normal. That is, they are neither "rational" nor "irrational."
2. People construct portfolios using behavioral portfolio theory, where their portfolios extend beyond high expected returns and low risk to include social responsibility and social status.
3. People save and spend according to behavioral life-cycle theory, where impediments like weak self-control make saving and spending appropriately difficult.
4. Behavioral asset pricing theory uses factors beyond risk to explain differences in expected returns.
5. Markets are efficient because they are hard to beat, not because price always equals value (Statman, 2019).

This chapter discusses some advances during the second generation of behavioral finance. Over this period, behavioral finance researchers have examined numerous areas. Because discussing them all is impractical, the following subsections highlight the five assertions mentioned above involving behavioral finance's second generation.

Behavioral decision-making

Standard finance assumes rational actors who don't make cognitive or emotional errors. However, Thaler (2015) and Statman (2017, 2019) view the central agents in the economy as human or normal, not the automatons depicted in conventional economic models. Real people are error-prone and succumb to behavioral biases. They use heuristics or shortcuts when making financial decisions. Hence, their beliefs and preferences filter a decision-maker's mental processes and can result in severe consequences. Normal people can make costly mistakes that differ from their best choices, solutions, and responses. Statman (2019, p. 7) notes, "The brains of rational people are never full. They can process information rapidly and accurately, free from cognitive and emotional errors. The brains of normal people, however, are often full." Thus, the second generation of behavioral finance provides a more accurate picture of ordinary people and their behavioral decision-making processes.

Behavioral portfolio theory

A central premise of standard finance is *modern portfolio theory* (MPT), based on the notion that a rational investor can build an optimal distribution of financial instruments within a portfolio that minimizes risk for a specific level of expected return. This rational investor is assumed to make every investment decision by evaluating each potential security in the framework of what it contributes to the portfolio. This theory provides an excellent starting point in the classroom for how people should make investment decisions. Behavioral finance academics have begun to offer a theory on how real people make decisions about their investment portfolios.

Shefrin and Statman (2000) apply mental accounting as the foundation for a behavioral portfolio theory (BPT) in which investors separate assets into mental accounts or categories, depending on their financial objectives. BPT identifies that individuals sometimes invest in suboptimal investment portfolios based on different goals (Ackert, 2014). For instance, a person with a set of financial objectives might have different levels of risk assessment for each goal. One financial objective could be to save for the down payment on a house within the next five years, whereas another could be to invest for retirement in 30 years. Someone with both goals has a different risk profile because of the different time horizons.

The person may be conservative by using money market instruments for the house down payment but aggressive by investing money in common stocks for the retirement account.

Statman (2019) extends the idea of financial goals to what investors want, such as a desire to avoid poverty, create wealth, raise children, and consider personal values. Furthermore, Statman (2019, p. 95) notes that behavioral portfolios can be described as goal-based portfolios. "Behavioral portfolios resemble layered pyramids, where each layer is dedicated to satisfying a want, often specified as a goal." An extension of how to implement Statman's layered pyramid or behavioral portfolio approach is to apply Maslow's hierarchy of needs theory of motivation (Maslow, 1943) within the financial planning process (Altfest, 2014; Crosby and Widger, 2012).

Maslow's hierarchy of needs is a model of human behavior for understanding an individual's motivation (Maslow, 1943). The model diagrams separate motivations placed on a layered pyramid, each layer symbolizing a different individual need. The different levels of need are physiological, safety, love and belongingness, self-esteem, and self-actualization. Crosby and Widger (2012) provide an overview of Brinker Capital's pyramid for assisting clients in achieving financial objectives. They assign investment funds to four categories – income, tactical, accumulation, and safety – corresponding with the ideas of BPT and the different levels of motivation associated with Maslow's hierarchy of needs.

Full implementation of a behavioral portfolio requires meeting with a financial planner to develop a comprehensive financial plan based on an extensive list of financial goals for the client. *Financial planning* is an approach that helps individuals develop a well-organized process for achieving their objectives. The financial planner must possess a certain level of expertise in behavioral finance to create a client financial plan that applies BPT's themes.

An additional improvement to applying BPT and Maslow's hierarchy of needs model within the financial planning process would be understanding the differences between financial coaching and financial therapy. The basis of *financial coaching* is solution-focused outcomes and tailoring positive results for each client to overcome biases and improve decisions based on financial outcomes and goals (Grable and Archuleta, 2014).

Financial therapy focuses on a deeper psychological experience throughout one's lifetime (Goetz and Gale, 2014). Money flashpoints (i.e., severe positive and negative childhood memories about money) and money beliefs (i.e., established viewpoints about money in adulthood) influence all clients. In severe cases, these money flashpoints and beliefs result in money disorders such as hoarding and compulsive gambling. Traditional financial planners or advisors would be most comfortable using behavioral coaching to improve their clients' financial outcomes. A referral to a financial therapist might be the best recommendation for the small percentage of clients incapable of accepting financial guidance or advice because of severe psychological trauma or potential money disorders.

Behavioral life-cycle theory

Another important tenet of standard finance is the *life-cycle theory* (LCT). It assumes that individuals optimize their current expenditures, assessing their spending needs and expected income over the rest of their lifespan (Modigliani, 1980). LCT assumes people are rational and forward-thinking. They are disposed to become planners who can maximize their financial resources during their lifetimes.

Behavioral finance offers a version known as *behavioral life-cycle theory* (BLCT). This model recognizes that implementing a rational spending approach over one's lifetime is difficult because people suffer from cognitive mistakes and affective issues (Shefrin and Thaler, 1988). At the center of these financial biases is balancing the desire to spend today versus the need to save for the future.

BLCT assumes that people suffer from *self-control bias*, the inclination causing them to fail to achieve their long-term financial objectives (e.g., saving for retirement) due to a lack of short-term discipline (e.g., impulsive overspending). In other words, many people are disposed to be spenders rather than savers or investors. They cannot sacrifice small, instant rewards for larger future rewards.

Mental accounting is another significant aspect of BLCT (Shefrin and Thaler, 1988). People engaging in mental accounting may separate their wealth into three mental accounts: (1) current income, (2) current assets, and (3) future income. Allocating funds to different mental categories results in conflicting financial objectives that might be detrimental to financial planning. In addition, individuals switch between short-term and long-term mental accounts to justify their current financial decisions. Therefore, a financial planner or advisor should implement a combination of the LCT and BLCT depending on whether a client is a rational investor, a behavioral investor, or a combination of both.

Behavioral asset pricing theory

Since the introduction of the capital asset pricing model (CAPM) in the early 1960s by William Sharpe, Jack Treynor, John Lintner, and Jan Mossin, researchers have developed and evaluated numerous multi-factor models for pricing stocks. Factor investing asserts that multiple independent sources of risk and return exist for stocks beyond *market beta*, defined as the risk and return attributable to investing in the stock market. Other models emerged that took non-risk characteristics into account. Some models were subject to substantial criticism involving *data mining*, a process used to extract usable data from more extensive raw data (Dowling and Lucey, 2017).

Fama and French (1993) introduced a three-factor model. This model specified that three factors explained most stock market returns: (1) risk as measured by the excess return on the market, (2) book-to-market values (value stocks tend to outperform), and (3) company size (smaller company stocks tend to outperform). Next came the Carhart four-factor model, which added an extra factor, called momentum, to the Fama–French three-factor model (Carhart, 1997). *Momentum* is the speed or velocity of price changes in a stock, security, or tradable instrument. Fama and French (2015) later modified their initial model to include five factors: the original three factors, plus "profitability" and "investment" factors. Numerous models currently seek to explain returns, using such factors as "quality," "low volatility," and "liquidity" (i.e., trading volume).

A limitation of these models is that they exclude behavioral factors and ignore culture. According to Dowling and Lucey (2017, p. 561), "… a need exists for much richer models of investor behavior and the social psychology of groups of investors." Such research may require using new behavioral and social datasets offered by online media to gain a more holistic understanding of the drivers of investment behavior. Thus, behavioral asset pricing is a future research area meriting attention. As Ibbotson et al. (2018, p. 31) note, "Although behavioral finance tells a rich story, it has thus far not provided a full framework or theory for understanding asset prices."

However, some researchers have incorporated behavioral factors into asset pricing models. For example, Shefrin and Statman (1994) developed a behavioral capital asset pricing theory. Statman et al. (2008) and Anginer and Statman (2010) incorporated affect into a behavioral asset pricing model. Statman and Glushkov (2011) developed a six-factor model consisting of the Fama–French–Carhart factors and two socially responsible factors. Ibbotson et al. (2018) have provided a more recent model. They developed the popular asset pricing model (PAPM), combining classical (standard) and behavioral finance elements. This model includes risks, frictions, and behavioral characteristics that help to explain most of the well-known premiums and anomalies. The authors contend that popularity, just another word for demand, is a bridge between classical and behavioral finance.

Behavioral efficient markets

Multiple approaches are available to explain the role of behavior in the financial markets. These approaches are contradictory and based on different assumptions. In standard finance, the dominant theory is the efficient market hypothesis (EMH), coined by University of Chicago economist and Nobel prize recipient Eugene Fama. Fama (1965, p. 56) explains market efficiency as follows: "... in an efficient market at any point in time the actual price of a security will be a good estimate of its value." This version of the EMH is the *price-equals-value EMH*, also called a value-efficient market. Its main assumptions concern perfect markets where no transaction costs exist, information is costless, and investors have homogenous expectations and are entirely rational. Based on these assumptions, investors perceive all available information similarly and incorporate all important information into current share prices. Thus, the market always prices a financial security correctly. Stocks are neither undervalued nor overvalued but trade at their fair or intrinsic value. Statman (2019, p. 141) states, "Value-efficient markets are impossible to beat because abnormal returns come from exploiting discrepancies between prices and values. Such discrepancies are absent in value-efficient markets." If a market is efficient, the investing world should be simple because the market truly knows best (Haugen, 2002; Shleifer, 2000).

Thus, there's no "free lunch" in financial markets. This approach was the dominant economic theory explaining financial markets for many years.

Behavioral finance challenges the assumptions of this theory, pointing out the market's inherent inefficiencies and investors' lack of rationality. Market inefficiencies exist due to information asymmetries, transaction costs, market psychology, human emotion, and other factors, causing prices to deviate from their true or intrinsic value. There is mixed empirical evidence concerning the notion of value-efficient markets (Kothari and Warner, 2007; Rau, 2010; Shleifer, 2000), with researchers documenting numerous anomalies inconsistent with the EMH (Ball, 2009). For example, if the assumptions underlying the price-equals-value EMH were correct, market bubbles would not exist. A *market bubble* is when prices rise rapidly, outpacing the true worth, or intrinsic value, of an asset, market sector, or industry. Additionally, investors do not always behave rationally, and stocks do not always trade at their fair value during financial crashes and crises because investors exhibit biases. Rau (2010, p. 333) notes, "However, even though these biases are systematic and predictable, limits to arbitrage prevent arbitrageurs from taking advantage of these biases and restoring market efficiency."

Another version of the EMH is the *hard-to-beat EMH* (Statman, 2019). In markets where such a hypothesis applies, some investors, especially professional investors like Warren Buffett and George Soros, can beat the market consistently and earn abnormal returns over time. Abnormal returns exceed those expected based on a correct asset pricing model. Such investors may be able to beat the market if they have exclusive information or narrowly available information that most investors do not have. Most investors cannot beat the market when using only widely available information and making cognitive and emotional errors unless they are lucky.

The many inconsistencies between the EMH and the empirical evidence led researchers to develop alternative concepts and theories. One such concept is the adaptive markets hypothesis (AMH) developed by Lo (2004, 2005, 2012, 2019). The *AMH* is a model combining EMH principles with those of behavioral finance. According to Lo (2004, p. 15), "… these two perspectives are opposite sides of the same coin." For example, the price-equals-value EMH assumes market participants are fully rational. Under the AMH, however, people are mainly rational but sometimes act irrationally, especially during periods of rapid change, economic shocks, and heightened market activity. Such irrationally leads to market anomalies and other situations inconsistent with the EMH. Another difference is that return predictability is impossible with the EMH but not with the AMH.

The AMH maintains that the theory of market efficiency is not wrong but incomplete. Lo (2004) asserts that individuals adapt to changing environments and apply evolutionary principles like competition, adaptation, and natural selection to financial interactions. The AMH assumes:

- People act in their self-interest, make mistakes, learn and adapt.
- Competition leads to adaptation and innovation, and natural selection shapes market ecology.
- This evolutionary process determines financial market dynamics.

The AMH has several implications. Market efficiency is not absolute but varies over time and across markets. For example, the market functions more efficiently when market participants are well adapted to the environment. However, it is less efficient when a shift in fundamentals occurs. Consequently, investment strategies can perform well in specific environments, leading to profit opportunities. A relationship exists between risk and return but it is unlikely to be stable over time due to different individual and institutional risk preferences (Plastun, 2017).

Although some empirical evidence supports the AMH (Neely et al., 2009; Kim et al., 2011; Zhou and Lee, 2013; Urquhart and McGroarty, 2014; Fahmy, 2018), Platsun (2017, p. 446), concludes that "More empirical research is required before the AMH can serve as a viable alternative to the EMH." Platsun also discusses other hypotheses used to explain the markets and their behavior, including the fractal market hypothesis, overreaction hypothesis, underreaction hypothesis, noisy market hypothesis, and functional fixation hypothesis. These hypotheses have behavioral components that help to explain the presence of anomalies. However, a general economic theory explaining financial market behavior remains elusive.

Summary and conclusions

Behavioral finance has entered its second generation. As behavioral decision-making, behavioral portfolio theory, behavioral life-cycle theory, behavioral asset pricing theory, and behavioral efficient markets attract more research, these topics will likely gain greater understanding and broader acceptance within academic finance. Addressing the many unanswered questions and unexplored opportunities will likely improve understanding of financial behavior.

References

Ackert, Lucy F. 2014. "Traditional and Behavioral Finance." In H. Kent Baker and Victor Ricciardi (eds.), *Investor Behavior: The Psychology of Financial Planning and Investing*, 25–41. Hoboken, NJ: John Wiley & Sons, Inc.

Altfest, Lewis J. 2014. "Motivation and Satisfaction." In H. Kent Baker and Victor Ricciardi (eds.), *Investor Behavior: The Psychology of Financial Planning and Investing*, 171–188. Hoboken, NJ: John Wiley & Sons, Inc.

Anginer, Deniz, and Meir Statman. 2010. "Stocks of Admired and Spurned Companies." *Journal of Portfolio Management* 36:3, 71–77.

Ball, Ray. 2009. "The Global Financial Crisis and the Efficient Market Hypothesis: What Have We Learned?" *Journal of Applied Corporate Finance* 21:4, 8–16.

Carhart, Mark M. 1997. "On Persistence in Mutual Fund Performance." *Journal of Finance* 52:1, 57–82.

Crosby, Daniel, and Chuck Widger. 2012. *Personal Benchmark: Integrating Behavioral Finance and Investment Management*. Hoboken, NJ: John Wiley & Sons, Inc.

Dowling, Michael, and Brian Lucey. 2017. "The Future of Behavioral Finance." In H. Kent Baker, Greg Filbeck, and Victor Ricciardi (eds.), *Financial Behavior: Payers, Services, Products, and Markets*, 561–578. New York: Oxford University Press.

Fahmy, Hany Ibrahim. 2018. "Testing the Empirical Validity of the Adaptive Markets Hypothesis." *Review of Economic Analysis* 9:2, 169–184.

Fama, Eugene F. 1965. "Random Walks in Stock Market Prices." *Financial Analysts Journal* 21:5, 55–59.

Fama, Eugene F., and Kenneth R. French. 1993. "Common Risk Factors in the Returns on Stocks and Bonds." *Journal of Financial Economics* 33:1, 3–56.

Fama, Eugene F., and Kenneth R. French. 2015. "A Five-Factor Asset Pricing Model." *Journal of Financial Economics* 116:1, 1–22.

Goetz, Joseph W., and Jerry E. Gale. 2014. "Financial Therapy: De-biasing and Client Behaviors." In H. Kent Baker and Victor Ricciardi (eds.), *Investor Behavior: The Psychology of Financial Planning and Investing*, 227–244. Hoboken, NJ: John Wiley & Sons, Inc.

Grable, John E., and Kristy L. Archuleta. 2014. "Financial Counseling and Coaching." In H. Kent Baker and Victor Ricciardi (eds.), *Investor Behavior: The Psychology of Financial Planning and Investing*, 209–226. Hoboken, NJ: John Wiley & Sons, Inc.

Haugen, Robert A. 2002. *The Inefficient Stock Market: What Pays Off and Why*, Second Edition. Upper Saddle River, NJ: Prentice Hall.

Ibbotson, Roger G., Thomas M. Idzorek, Paul D. Kaplan, and James X. Xiong. 2018. *Popularity: A Bridge between Classical and Behavioral Finance*. Charlottesville, VA: CFA Institute Research Foundation.

Kim, Jae H., Abdul Shamsuddin, and Kian-Ping Lim. 2011. "Stock Return Predictability and the Adaptive Markets Hypothesis: Evidence from Century-Long U.S. Data?" *Journal of Empirical Finance* 8:5, 868–879.

Kothari, S. P., and Jerold B. Warner. 2007. "Econometrics of Event Studies." In B. Espen Eckbo (ed.), *Handbook of Corporate Finance: Empirical Corporate Finance*, 3–36. Amsterdam: North-Holland.

Lo, Andrew S. 2004. "The Adaptive Markets Hypothesis: Market Efficiency from an Evolutionary Perspective." *Journal of Portfolio Management* 30:5, 15–29.

Lo, Andrew W. 2005. "Reconciling Efficient Markets with Behavioral Finance: The Adaptive Markets Hypothesis." *Journal of Investment Consulting* 7:2, 21–44.

Lo, Andrew W. 2012. "Adaptive Markets and the New World Order." *Financial Analysts Journal* 68:2, 18–28.

Lo, Andrew W. 2019. *Adaptive Markets: Financial Evolution at the Speed of Thought*, Second Edition. Princeton, NJ: Princeton University Press.

Maslow, Abraham H. 1943. "A Theory of Human Motivation." *Psychological Review* 50:4, 370–396.

Modigliani, Franco. 1980. "The Life Cycle Hypothesis of Saving." In *The Collected Papers of Franco Modigliani*, Volume 2. Cambridge, MA: MIT Press.

Neely, Christopher J., Paul A. Weller, and Joshua Ulrich. 2009. "The Adaptive Markets Hypothesis: Evidence from the Foreign Exchange Market." *Journal of Financial and Quantitative Analysis* 42:2, 467–488.

Plastun, Alex. 2017. "Behavioral Finance Market Hypotheses." In H. Kent Baker, Greg Filbeck, and Victor Ricciardi (eds.), *Financial Behavior: Players, Services, Products, and Markets*, 439–459. New York: Oxford University Press.

Rau, Raghavendra. 2010. "Market Inefficiency." In H. Kent Baker and John R. Nofsinger (eds.), *Behavioral Finance: Investors, Corporations, and Markets*, 333–349. Hoboken, NJ: John Wiley & Sons, Inc.

Shefrin, Hersh, and Meir Statman. 1994. "Behavioral Capital Asset Pricing Theory." *Journal of Financial and Quantitative Analysis* 29:3, 323–349.

Shefrin, Hersh, and Meir Statman. 2000. "Behavioral Portfolio Theory." *Journal of Financial and Quantitative Analysis* 35:2, 127–151.

Shefrin, Hersh, and Richard Thaler. 1988. "The Behavioral Life-Cycle Hypothesis." *Economic Inquiry* 26:4, 609–643.

Shleifer, Andrei. 2000. *Inefficient Markets: An Introduction to Behavioral Finance*. New York: Oxford University Press.

Statman, Meir. 2017. *Finance for Normal People: How Investors and Markets Behave*. New York: Oxford University Press.

Statman, Meir. 2019. *Behavioral Finance: The Second Generation.* Charlottesville, VA: CFA Institute Research Foundation.

Statman, Meir, Kenneth L. Fisher, and Deniz Anginer. 2008. "Affect in a Behavioral Asset-Pricing Model." *Financial Analysts Journal* 64:2, 20–29.

Statman, Meir, and Denys Glushkov. 2011. "A Behavioral Asset Pricing Model with Social Responsibility Factors." Working Paper (November 18).

Thaler, Richard H. 2015. *Misbehaving: The Making of Behavioral Economics.* New York and London: W. W. Norton & Company.

Urquhart, Andrew, and Frank McGroarty. 2014. "Calendar Effects, Market Conditions and the Adaptive Market Hypothesis: Evidence from Long-Run U.S. Data." *International Review of Financial Analysis* 35:1, 154–166.

Zhou, Jian, and Jin Man Lee. 2013. "Adaptive Market Hypothesis: Evidence from the REIT Market." *Applied Financial Economics* 23:21, 1649–1662.

11 Behavioral finance moving forward

The future of behavioral finance requires understanding more about its philosophy, gaining a deeper understanding of the drivers of financial behavior, and ensuring rigorous research.
–Michael Dowling and Brian Lucey (2017, p. 561)

Introduction

Over the past several decades, a transformation has occurred from the traditional finance paradigm to a new approach – behavioral finance (Cronqvist and Jiang, 2017). This evolution continues. As Tomer (2017, p. 148) observes, "New research results in the discovery of new truths and leads to new perspectives." However, behavioral finance is not without critics or challenges. Legitimate disagreement exists about behavioral finance and its future. Although some are critical of its current state, they still recognize the astonishing progress already made (Dowling and Lucey, 2017). For example, behavioral finance has significantly contributed to understanding anomalous financial behaviors, how financial markets work, behavioral aspects of people's financial decisions, and the design of frameworks to nudge people into making better decisions. Much still needs to be learned and applied to actual situations. The remainder of this chapter discusses some challenges and opportunities facing behavioral finance.

Behavioral finance challenges

Behavioral finance faces several challenges. Meeting them could help shape its future. Below are three criticisms about behavioral finance that represent challenges to moving forward unless appropriately addressed.

Integrating standard and behavioral finance

Crosby (2013) states that a need exists to integrate behavioral finance into the standard finance fabric. Historically, these two schools of financial thought have needlessly been at odds. This apparent conflict stemmed from behavioral finance proponents wanting to advance their ideas by concentrating on areas where traditional finance was deficient. However, taking a combative approach is not helpful when solving practical problems. Each side has something to offer.

A better mindset views traditional and behavioral finance as complements, not substitutes. Hence, the challenge is to combine evidence from both camps in applied ways to improve the financial decision-making of individuals, groups, and organizations. As Davies and Brooks (2017, p. 544) note: "Behavioral finance should help make traditional finance more relevant because it shows how to relax the overly narrow normative assumptions to adapt these models to the real world, providing better solutions for real people."

Developing a more unified theory of behavioral finance

Another criticism of behavioral finance is that many empirical results lack a theoretical foundation (Mittal, 2022). Thus, more theoretical studies could deliver beneficial results. Behavioral finance also lacks a unified theory (Shleifer, 2000, p. 25). This situation is common in other fields as a new body of theory and empirical evidence emerges. As Szyszka (2010, p. 351) notes, "… behavioral finance is affected by an ailment typical of relatively young and scarcely penetrated areas of knowledge. That is, a plethora of research carried out in an uncoordinated manner produced fragmentary outcomes that are difficult to unite in a comprehensive theory."

Initial efforts in behavioral finance focused on small models or theories dealing with relevant issues facing decision-makers. However, Statman

(2019, p. ix) notes, "... today's standard finance is no longer unified because wide cracks have opened between the theory that it embraces and the evidence." After decades of research, a large body of knowledge has emerged on behavioral finance. This situation offers the opportunity to develop a comprehensive theory describing all the fundamental forces and relationships in a theoretical framework. Statman (2017) and others have taken steps in that direction. He offers a unified structure of behavioral finance, incorporating parts of standard finance, replacing others, and including bridges between theory, evidence, and practice. Statman (2017, p. xiv) notes, "Behavioral finance, and finance more generally, is a mosaic. Each tile matters, but a unified image emerges only when the mosaic tiles complement one another." However, behavioralists have not yet developed a coherent model that predicts the future rather than merely explaining it. The future of behavioral finance will see further attempts to develop a more unified structure.

However, some view any attempts to seek a perfect model of applied behavioral finance as unrealistic. Davies and Brooks (2017, p. 545) make the following observation.

> Any quest for a grand unified theory to mirror that of physical sciences may well be entirely misguided, together with the notion that such a theory is necessary for the broad field to be helpful. A much more effective approach is to treat the full range of behavioral findings as a rich toolbox that can be applied to and tested on a range of practical concerns.

Achieving a "perfect" model in any social science is unrealistic. However, continually refining theories and models to create a more unified structure is a proper function for behavioral finance scholars.

Incorporating behavioral finance concepts into practice

A third criticism of behavioral finance is that it is "... not sufficiently developed and coherent to be practically useful" (Davies and Brooks, 2017, p. 544). Practitioners compromise behavioral finance's effectiveness if applied superficially. Thus, practitioners face the challenge of building a bridge between behavioral finance theory and practice.

For example, behavioral finance is challenging for investment advisors to execute successfully. According to Swan Global Investments (2020), advisors face three main challenges. First, investors fail to see the value in behavioral coaching. A *financial coach* is a trained professional who collaborates with and guides clients to reach their financial goals. Such professionals know that behavioral biases often inhibit investors from making sound financial decisions, especially when their emotions are high. Although behavioral finance research provides lengthy lists of biases, few frameworks are available for financial practitioners to use when facing client problems. Thus, they often offer a checklist of biases hoping that simply informing their clients of them improves poor decision-making. Because few standardized instruments or tests are available to identify specific client biases, the burden falls on the shoulders of the financial coach or advisor.

Although financial coaching is vital to any advisor–client relationship, a recent Morningstar survey shows a difference between what investors value from their advisors and what advisors believe investors value (Lamas et al., 2019). For example, investors place far less importance on having financial advisors keeping them on track and helping them control their emotions than advisors believe necessary. As Lamas et al. (2019, p. 2) note, "This disconnect creates problems on both sides of the relationship. For advisors, it's hard to build a mutually beneficial relationship if clients don't understand the value of the advice they're getting." The challenge is identifying how to change investors' perceptions to get investors and advisors on the same page.

A second challenge in applying behavioral finance to wealth and investment management is that the investment industry engages in contradictory behavior. It emphasizes achieving long-term goals while encouraging biased behavior by over-emphasizing short-term returns and benchmark performance. The attention placed on meeting or beating the market reinforces the fixation on returns instead of goals. Thus, the industry reinforces a short-term investor mindset by stressing gains over goals. Consequently, investors overvalue short-term performance and devalue financial advice focusing on long-term value. Financial advisors will have difficulty successfully implementing behavioral finance with their clients unless the investment industry redefines how it views returns, planning, and advice.

A final challenge is a failure to incorporate the fear of losing money (loss aversion) at the portfolio level. A critical emotional driver of investment decisions is that investors do not want to lose money. When markets are up, investors are likely to follow their plans, but they often succumb to emotional biases and abandon them when markets are down. Thus, the core of portfolio construction should focus on creating a portfolio that reduces volatility by managing risk to achieve a goal rather than emphasizing gains.

Behavioral finance opportunities

Behavioral finance has many opportunities for continued growth and development at the micro and macro levels. Researchers have not developed solutions for all the problems they study. Additionally, there is a lack of theoretical explanations for some results. Although no one has a crystal ball to predict behavioral finance's future direction, the following opportunities and research areas may yield promising results.

Shifting toward value-based finance

Finance does not stand still but continues to evolve. For example, a developing school of thought is *value-based finance*, which incorporates one's belief system, including ethics, morals, and religion, into decision-making. This approach examines the environmental and social impact of a company's leaders, actions, and products. Value-based finance should not be confused with *value investing*, an investment paradigm involving buying securities that appear underpriced using some form of fundamental analysis.

Value-based finance shares features with socially responsible investing (SRI), corporate social responsibility (CSR), sustainable investing, impact investing, and social finance. Using a value-based lens for decision-making, many investors and companies want to build wealth but not at the expense of their values. They have dual objectives: making money and doing good. Such investors want to make money mean more. The movement toward value-based finance represents another paradigm shift. Researchers must determine how investors can best meet financial and non-financial objectives.

According to Hirshleifer (2015, p. 144), behavioral finance needs to shift into *social finance*, which includes "the study of how social norms, moral attitudes, religions and ideologies affect financial behaviors … and how ideologies that affect financial decisions form and spread." Such research would draw on social psychology and sociology plus cognitive psychology and decision theory and focus on the microstructure of social transactions. Analyzing social interactions could lead to a better understanding of the origin of heuristics, shifts in investor sentiment, and the causes and consequences of financial bubbles and crises.

Increasing the focus on behavioral corporate finance

Behavioral finance initially focused on irrational investors and inefficient markets but eventually included behavioral corporate finance (BCF). Corporate managers are also human and subject to irrational behavior. Such analysis often concentrates on how a chief executive officer's characteristics, such as overconfidence and optimism, introduce biases affecting a firm's financial decision-making. However, the CEO plays a small role in a firm's overall direction (Quigley and Hambrick, 2015). Dowling and Lucey (2017) suggest widening the scope of this analysis to include top management teams and the institutional influences on corporate decisions. They also stress the need for integrating more organizational theory into BCF.

Another gap in current BCF research involves identifying cultural differences and behavioral biases that influence corporate financial decisions worldwide. Lucey and Dowling (2014) stress that cross-cultural differences, mainly social, exist in various corporate finance behaviors. However, cognitive biases also differ across countries. Therefore, a need exists for more research in BCF in a global context. Dowling and Lucey (2017, p. 569) conclude, "International studies need to determine appropriate interactions between cultural effects and psychological influences on corporate financial decision making."

A third BCF topic meriting further study is the effect of activist campaigns by hedge funds and others on the behavior of executives and boards. Does such activism help to correct the behavioral mistakes of managers? How do top management and boards respond to activist challenges? Do they dismiss activist ideas, fend off such challenges, or use them to improve their organizations? How does such managerial behavior affect the firm's short- and long-run financial performance and its stakeholders? All these questions merit additional study.

Understanding the drivers of financial behavior

Behavioral finance has revealed many intriguing insights about how people approach money. Research shows that people are psychologically hardwired to behave in predictable ways. The behavior driving their financial decisions extends well beyond the numbers because money is an emotionally charged topic. Financial decisions reflect biases, emotions, cognitive errors, values, and goals. Financial knowledge, literacy, and attitude also play a role.

What is the source of this hardwiring? Is it nature or nurture? Some people exhibit specific behavioral biases, while others show different preferences. Much literature studies the relative importance of learning (i.e., nurture) versus biology (nature) in financial decision-making (Nofsinger and Shank, 2020). Scientists have mapped the human genome, providing an opportunity to discover how biology affects behavioral finance.

Although researchers have made considerable progress identifying drivers of financial behavior, a catalyst meriting additional research is the impact of culture on financial decision-making. Researchers also need to understand the key motivators of economic behavior and create behavioral financial strategies to reflect individuals with different drivers. Such a framework would enable advisors to help their clients negotiate the psychological and mechanical aspects of their finances and improve their decision-making.

Addressing the challenges of applying behavioral finance

Many studies reveal successful applications of behavioral finance. These applications include strategies used by financial advisors to help their clients avoid behavioral errors, enabling them to make better decisions (Evensky, 2017). Another example involves using nudges to address specific problems to improve behavior, such as making better financial decisions related to saving more, investing more wisely, diversifying more effectively, and choosing better insurance plans and credit cards (Thaler and Bernartzi, 2004; Thaler and Sunstein, 2008). *Nudging*, also known as *libertarian paternalism*, is any attempt to influence someone's judgment, choice, or behavior in a predictable way (Thaler and Sunstein, 2003). As Benjamin Graham, the father of value investing, once noted, "The investor's chief problem – and even his worst enemy – is likely to be himself." Thus, nudges can help people make better choices to improve their welfare. Nevertheless, many examples of ineffective nudges and failed attempts to implement behavioral finance exist (Sunstein, 2017). Researchers must identify the factors associated with effective good nudges before applying them.

Nudges can also have an evil or dark side if used with bad intentions. Naming the "evil" side with a word like "sludge" can debunk abuses without letting them be associated with the original "nudge for good" concept (Mantashian, 2018). Financial firms and advisors should use their knowledge and expertise to advise on and recommend suitable financial products in their client's best interests. However, some use nudges primarily for profit, resulting in customer exploitation. For example, commission-based advisors could use nudges to influence clients to buy more financial products, generating higher fees and sales incentives for the advisor (Cheng, 2020). Another example of dark nudges is selling overly complex and poor value-for-money products to consumers, such as subprime mortgages with ballooning interest rates. These bad or dark nudges deserve additional research because they can lead to significant losses in welfare (Albrecht, 2018). In summary, nudges can help steer people toward decisions that benefit or manipulate them.

Davies and Brooks (2017) note that the rigorous academic research underpinning behavioral finance offers many valuable untapped insights. Still, implementing behavioral finance involves practical challenges, including using superficial approaches, transferring academic findings to a real-world environment, tailoring the problem and environment, and overcoming reluctance to embrace behaviorally grounded methods despite evidence supporting their effectiveness. Fields like behavioral economics are seductive because they promise people easy, cookie-cutter solutions to complicated problems. Researchers must identify impediments to successful implementation and develop strategies to overcome them. For example, merely informing people of their biases or errors is seldom effective in overcoming them. Thus, researchers need to focus on converting ideas successfully into positive outcomes.

Building behavioral asset pricing models

Standard and behavioral finance approaches to asset pricing models have similarities and differences. Standard finance makes strong assumptions, but many are unrealistic. However, such assumptions are necessary to develop testable mathematical formulas using market data. These models are normative. Unfortunately, actual market observations often diverge from predictions from financial theory. By contrast, behavioral finance asset pricing models are generally more intuitive and less formal, making them difficult to test empirically. Behavioral models can explain market anomalies *ex post* but encounter difficulty when used for *ex ante* predictions. Szyszka (2010, p. 351) notes, "Any theory is only as good as its ability to explain or predict the processes actually taking place."

Statman (2019, p. 140) offers the following observations about standard and behavioral asset pricing models.

> Behavioral asset pricing models, like standard asset pricing models, are factor or characteristic models that either begin with theoretical rationales for factors and characteristics or strive to identify theoretical rationales for factors and characteristics found empirically. Behavioral asset pricing models and standard asset pricing models differ in the breadth of theoretical rationales. Theoretical rationales in behavioral asset pricing models encompass wants for utilitarian, expressive, and emotional benefits and the presence of cognitive and emotional errors, whereas theoretical rationales in standard asset pricing models are limited to wants for utilitarian benefits – mainly low risk and high expected returns – and feature an absence of cognitive and emotional errors.

Despite considerable progress, both approaches are "works in progress" (Statman, 2019, p. 140). Chapter 1 notes that the list of factors has grown from one in the capital asset pricing model (CAPM) to three, four, five, and more in other models. Researchers have made much progress based on behavioral capital asset pricing theory (Shefrin and Statman, 1994). Other researchers set forth belief-based (Barberis et al., 1998; Daniel et al., 1998; Hong and Stein, 1999) and preference-based (Barberis et al., 2001; Dacey and Zielonka, 2008) models. Szyszka (2010) proposed a generalized behavioral model. Yet, more work is needed to identify the theoretical rationales for factors.

Improving the reliability of behavioral finance research

A final opportunity in behavioral finance is to improve the research reliability. Baker et al. (2019) note fundamental differences between research in psychology and research in finance. For example, experimental and survey-based methods are far more common in psychology than finance. Often these approaches rely on proprietary data. Using such methods may lead to questioning the results' reliability and robustness. Although such procedures offer advantages, such as controlling the variables and determining cause and effect relations, they also have limitations. For instance, subjects know they are part of an experiment, potentially producing unnatural behavior. Using a small or nonrepresentative sample could make generalizing the findings to the population difficult. These methods typically focus on the behavior of individuals, not markets. By contrast, financial researchers generally use databases available to other researchers, enabling replication of their results. However, databases on individual investors are often private. More data on individual investors must become available to researchers while maintaining the confidentiality of the data source and investor identities.

Several avenues are available to improve the reliability of behavioral finance research. As Dowling and Lucey (2017) note, such research requires reliable theory and appropriate methodologies that stand up to rigorous replication. Additionally, journals should ask their authors to provide their datasets and methodology files.

Summary and conclusions

Behavioral finance continues progressing, but its work is far from complete. Statman (2019, p. 175) states, "Behavioral finance is still under construction today." It faces both challenges and opportunities. Where is behavioral finance headed? Although the answer to this question is speculative, this book provides some clues.

References

Albrecht, Leslie. 2018. "How Behavioral Economics Is Being Used against You." *MarketWatch*, June 17. Available at https://www.marketwatch.com/story/nob-el-prize-winning-economist-richard-thalers-nudge-theory-has-a-dark-side-too-2017-10-17.

Baker, H. Kent, Greg Filbeck, and John R. Nofsinger. 2019. *Behavioral Finance: What Everyone Needs to Know.* New York: Oxford University Press.

Barberis, Nicholas, Ming Huang, and Tano Santos. 2001. "Prospect Theory and Asset Prices." *Quarterly Journal of Economics* 116:1, 1–53.

Barberis, Nicholas, Andrei Shleifer, and Robert Vishny. 1998. "A Model of Investor Sentiment." *Journal of Financial Economics* 49:3, 307–343.

Cheng, Sara. 2020. "The Power of Nudges in Financial Advice." *Market Integrity Insights*, CFA Institute, October 21. Available at https://blogs.cfainstitute.org/marketintegrity/2020/10/21/the-power-of-nudges-in-financial-advice/.

Cronqvist, Henrik, and Danling Jiang. 2017. "Individual Investors." In H. Kent Baker, Greg Filbeck, and Victor Ricciardi (eds.), *Financial Behavior: Players, Services, Products, and Markets*, 45–63. New York: Oxford University Press.

Crosby, Daniel. 2013. "Behavioral Finance Is Dead?" *InvestmentNews*, October 17. Available at https://www.investmentnews.com/behavioral-finance-is-dead-54494.

Dacey, Raymond, and Piotr Zielonka. 2008. "A Detailed Prospect Theory Explanation of the Disposition Effect." *Journal of Behavioral Finance* 9:1, 43–50.

Daniel, Kent, David Hirshleifer, and Avanidhar Subrahmanyam. 1998. "Investor Psychology and Security Market Under- and Overreactions." *Journal of Finance* 53:6, 1839–1885.

Davies, Greg B., and Peter Brooks. 2017. "Practical Challenges of Implementing Behavioral Finance." In H. Kent Baker, Greg Filbeck, and Victor Ricciardi (eds.), *Financial Behavior: Payers, Services, Products, and Markets*, 542–560. New York: Oxford University Press.

Dowling, Michael, and Brian Lucey. 2017. "The Future of Behavioral Finance." In H. Kent Baker, Greg Filbeck, and Victor Ricciardi (eds.), *Financial Behavior: Payers, Services, Products, and Markets*, 561–578. New York: Oxford University Press.

Evensky, Harold. 2017. "Applications of Client Behavior." In H. Kent Baker, Greg Filbeck, and Victor Ricciardi (eds.), *Financial Behavior: Payers, Services, Products, and Markets*, 523–541. New York: Oxford University Press.

Hirshleifer, David (2015). "Behavioral Finance." *Annual Review of Financial Economics* 7, 133–159.

Hong, Harrison, and Jeremy C. Stein. 1999. "A Unified Theory of Underreaction, Momentum Trading and Overreaction in Asset Markets." *Journal of Finance* 54:6, 2143–2184.

Lamas, Samantha, Ryan O. Murphy, and Ray Sin. 2019. "The Value of Advice: What Investors Think, What Advisors Think, and How Everyone Can Get on the Same Page." Morningstar, Inc. Available at https://www.morningstar.com/content/dam/marketing/shared/pdfs/InvestorSuccessProject/value-of-advice/value-of-advice.pdf?utm_source=eloqua&utm_medium=email&utm_campaign=none&utm_content=16143.

Lucey, Brian M., and Michael Dowling. 2014. "Cultural Behavioral Finance in Emerging Markets." In Mohamed Hedi Arouri, Sabri Boubaker, and Duc Nguyen (eds.), *Emerging Markets and the Global Economy*, 327–346. Amsterdam: Elsevier.

Mantashian, Jenic. 2018. "Nudge, Dark Nudges, Sludge and Dealing with the Ethics of BE." BVA Nudge Unit, October 23. Available at https://bvanudgeunit.com/nudge-dark-nudge-sludge-dealing-with-ethics-be/.

Mittal, Satish K. 2022. "Behavior Biases and Investment Decision: Theoretical and Research Framework." *Qualitative Research in Financial Markets* 14:2, 213–228.

Nofsinger, John R., and Corey Shank. 2020. *The Biology of Investing: Nature, Nurture, Physiology, and Cognition*. New York: Routledge.

Quigley, Timothy J., and Donald C. Hambrick. 2015. "Has the 'CEO Effect' Increased in Recent Decades? A New Explanation for the Great Rise in America's Attention to Corporate Leaders." *Strategic Management Journal* 36:6, 821–830.

Shefrin, Hersh, and Meir Statman. 1994. "Behavioral Capital Asset Pricing Theory." *Journal of Financial and Quantitative Analysis* 29:3, 323–349.

Shleifer, Andrei. 2000. *Inefficient Markets: An Introduction to Behavioral Finance.* Oxford: Oxford University Press.

Statman, Meir. 2017. *Finance for Normal People: How Investors and Markets Behave.* New York: Oxford University Press.

Statman, Meir. 2019. *Behavioral Finance: The Second Generation.* Charlottesville, VA: CFA Institute Research Foundation.

Sunstein, Cass R. 2017. "Nudges that Fail." *Behavioural Public Policy* 1:1, 4–25.

Swan Global Investments. 2020. "Why Behavioral Finance Is Challenging for Advisors to Execute Successfully." January 1. Available at https://www .etftrends.com/etf-strategist-channel/why-behavioral-finance-is-challenging -for-advisors-to-execute-successfully/.

Szyszka, Adam. 2010. "Belief- and Preference-Based Models." In H. Kent Baker and John R. Nofsinger (eds.), *Behavioral Finance: Investors, Corporations, and Markets*, 351–372. Hoboken, NJ: John Wiley & Sons, Inc.

Thaler, Richard H., and Shlomo Benartzi. 2004. "Save More Tomorrow: Using Behavioral Economics to Increase Employee Saving." *Journal of Political Economy* 112:1, 164–187.

Thaler, Richard H., and Cass R. Sunstein. 2003. "Libertarian Paternalism." *American Economic Review* 93:2, 175–179.

Thaler, Richard H., and Cass R. Sunstein. 2008. *Nudge: Improving Decisions about Health, Wealth, and Happiness.* New Haven, CT: Yale University Press.

Tomer, John F. 2017. *Advanced Introduction to Behavioral Economics.* Cheltenham, U.K. and Northampton, MA, U.S.A.: Edward Elgar Publishing.

Index

Titles in the **Elgar Advanced Introductions** series include: